Circling the Wolf's Head

People often remark that the outline of Lake Superior, when viewed on a map or from the upper reaches of the earth's atmosphere, resembles the profile of a wolf's head, with the Keweenaw Peninsula forming the wolf's mouth, and Isle Royale its eye.

Circling the Wolf's Head
Travels and Encounters around Lake Superior

Robert Eaton

Printed in the United States of America

ISBN 979-8-9886111-0-3 (KDP hardcover)
ISBN 979-8-9886111-1-0 (KDP paperback)
ISBN 979-8-9886111-2-7 (Kindle e-book)

Library of Congress Control Number: 2023916538

The photograph of Pictured Rocks National Lakeshore, Michigan, on the front cover is from iStock LP (Stock file ID #1320407667) and is used under iStock's standard license.

The Moderate Resolution Image Spectroradiometer (MODIS) image of Lake Superior on the frontispiece is courtesy of the National Aeronautics and Space Administration and the National Oceanic and Atmospheric Administration and shows the lake on September 7, 2022.

To the memory of my parents, and for JLH

Contents

Preface

Lake Superior is the largest, deepest, coldest, and purest of North America's Great Lakes. Covering an area the size of Maine, it is the world's most extensive freshwater body and in places reaches a depth of over thirteen hundred feet. At its normal level the lake contains more than three quadrillion gallons of water—that's 3,000,000,000,000,000 gallons—and each day discharges fifty billion gallons of water to Lake Huron (and, ultimately, the Saint Lawrence River and the Atlantic Ocean) through the Saint Mary's River, enough to meet the drinking, cooking, and bathing needs of every human now living on the planet, if only it were economical to capture, transport, and distribute it.

Lake Superior straddles the international border between the United States and Canada in the middle of the North American continent, and its climate is, to put it politely, extreme. During cold winters, like the winter of 1995-96, its entire surface freezes. (Imagine: an ice rink the size of Maine.) And even during warm summers only its shallows are comfortably swimmable. Because of its short growing season and lack of arable soils—glaciers scoured the area—the Lake Superior basin supports little agriculture, and only six hundred thousand people live within its boundary. As a result, the lake itself is nearly pristine; in many places one can still safely drink its untreated water.

The storms and swells on Lake Superior, an inland sea that can generate its own weather, are notoriously unpredictable, and navigation on it can be treacherous. Since the advent of large-scale commercial shipping on the lake in 1855, when the first locks were constructed at Sault Sainte Marie, Michigan, enabling large ships to traverse between Superior and the lower Great Lakes, the lake has claimed more than 350 ships, including, most famously (thanks to Gordon Lightfoot's haunting, memorable song), the SS *Edmund Fitzgerald*, a seven-hundred-foot-long ore freighter that disappeared in a gale in November 1975 with its crew of twenty-nine men.

Enough data and facts. Lake Superior is undoubtedly a remarkable natural resource and geographic feature, but if one is looking for more impressive statistics about it, one should look elsewhere. This book is not intended to be a compendium of information about the lake, or a comprehensive natural or cultural history of the lake and its environs, or even a travel guide to the area. Rather, it is simply my attempt to describe my personal experiences while traveling in the Lake Superior region over the course of several years beginning in the late 1990s.

Because I don't live in the region, my experiences were necessarily limited by the amount of time I was able to spend there and the other vagaries of travel, and consequently my observations will strike some people as limited, arbitrary, or biased. In response, all I can say is that we suffer—each of us—

from the same disability, if I may call it that, in that we perceive the world from a perspective that is uniquely our own, a perspective informed by our knowledge and judgment; colored by our emotions, expectations, and prejudices; and constrained by the time and other resources we are able to devote to a subject. As a result, each of us is limited in different ways. Granted, a visitor may never gain the deep knowledge of a place—or develop the deep emotional attachment to it—that a lifelong resident has. But a visitor who is curious and open-minded and who attempts to faithfully capture in words his or her admittedly limited and subjective experience may nevertheless contribute something of value to the collective wisdom of the place. At least that's my hope and belief. That is also, of course, the premise underlying most travel writing.

* * *

Lake Superior is stunningly beautiful and geographically remote and is for many people a symbol of wildness and purity, and for that reason alone it had attracted my interest for many years before I visited the area to work on this book. But the lake's obvious allure doesn't entirely explain the genesis of this project. There are many wonderful places in the world, and all of them are, or would be, worth writing about. In order for me to explain why I undertook to write a book about Lake Superior, I need to dwell for a few minutes on my family history, here at the beginning of the book, as I will in the last chapter, at the end.

My father was a career naval officer, and when I was growing up, our family led the peripatetic life of the military family, moving from duty station to duty station every two or three years. My father's father had also been a career naval officer, and when my father was growing up, in the late 1920s and 1930s, his family likewise had moved from place to place—from Charleston, South Carolina, to Norfolk, Virginia, to Shanghai, China, to Buffalo, New York, to Long Beach, California, to Honolulu, Hawaii. We are, or were, a deracinated lot.

But my grandfather had grown up somewhere and was from someplace, and that place was Duluth, Minnesota, at the western end of Lake Superior. His father—my great-grandfather—had settled in Duluth in the late 1890s, during the city's boom years, and become a successful businessman, prominent local politico, and colorful man-about-town. The family lived in a comfortable house near the bustling downtown and was by all accounts active and prominent in local society. By the time my father was born, in 1922, my grandfather had embarked on his naval career, and my father himself never lived in Duluth. But he learned about Duluth from his father's stories about growing up there and his family's occasional visits, and the city acquired for him a significance out of all proportion to the time he spent there. Years later, when my father talked about Duluth, I could tell from his reverential tone that it represented for him an elusive and almost mythical homeland: Odysseus's Ithaca, Inman's Cold Mountain.

When I was nine or ten years old, my father's aunt Mildred—his father's sister—and her husband, Otto, drove from Duluth to Norfolk, Virginia, to visit us. Mil and my grandfather had been the only two children in their family who had survived into adulthood, and since my grandfather had been killed in World War II, my father was extraordinarily fond of his aunt, who was the sole surviving member of that earlier generation and who represented a living link to his father, and to Duluth.

Mil and Ottie brought with them tantalizing stories of Duluth and Lake Superior; of rivers, waterfalls, and a freshwater lake larger than any I had ever seen (or could imagine); of canoes, sailboats, and freighters; of gales and blizzards; agates and iron ore.

They also brought me a copy of *Paddle-to-the-Sea*, Holling Clancy Holling's strangely affecting tale of an Indian boy in the Nipigon Country north of Lake Superior who one winter whittles a small figurine of an Indian in a canoe and on the bottom of the canoe carves the words "PLEASE PUT ME BACK IN WATER. I AM PADDLE TO THE SEA." The boy places the figurine on a snowdrift overlooking a river. The spring snowmelt carries the figurine down the river and into Nipigon Bay, and from there Paddle floats or is carried around Lake Superior, through the locks at Sault Sainte Marie, down the lower Great Lakes and the Saint Lawrence Seaway, and into the Atlantic Ocean. During his four-year journey he is nearly destroyed by a sawmill; survives severe winter storms, a forest fire (while lodged on a small island near the shore), near-collisions with Great Lakes freighters, and the plummet over Niagara Falls; and is rescued or repaired and returned to the water by the various people who find him. Finally, while floating in the ocean near the Grand Banks of Newfoundland, he is netted by a boy on a French fishing boat and carried to France. In the end, the Indian boy who made him, now a young man, overhears two men on a dock in the Nipigon country discussing a newspaper story about Paddle. "I made that one," he says softly, before turning, walking to the end of the dock, and paddling away in his own canoe.

I was enthralled by the tale, and thereafter Duluth and Lake Superior acquired for me a status akin to what they held for my father. But I didn't come to know the city, and the larger region in which it is located, until I was middle-aged and beginning to do the research for this book. During my numerous visits over the next ten years I met my various relatives in town and became good friends with one of my cousins, and for that reason alone I now feel lucky to have undertaken this idiosyncratic project. I also feel lucky to have had the opportunity to visit and learn about a place that members of my family have called home for several generations, a place that has loomed large in my family's shared memories and folklore.

During my visits I also became acquainted with the region's distinctive modern culture—for convenience I'll call it the North Woods frontier culture—one that seems to be shared today, in one form or another, by all who live there (native and nonnative alike) and that seems to embrace and embody the region's natural environment—its harsh climate, rugged beauty, abundant wildlife, valuable mineral and timber resources, remoteness from centers of human population, and the significant challenges it presents (and has always presented) to year-round human habitation. It is a culture in which the elemental forces of nature still figure prominently.

My visits to the area also reminded me that history is not something that happened only in the past, and not something produced only by those who accomplished great feats (or are credited with accomplishing great feats) and whose images are preserved in stylized form in our cultural memory, like the remarkable impressions of ancient ferns in a bed of shale. Rather, it is an ongoing, accretive process, and we are all a part of it. Although history will not remember each of us individually, we contribute—all of us—to the rich, layered sediment that will become the historical record. We become the matrix surrounding those fossilized ferns. And so this book includes not only information about the great historical figures who explored or settled the Lake Superior region in the past, but also sketches of the people I encountered during my contemporary travels— people ordinary by historical standards, perhaps, but remarkable and wonderful in their own way. They enriched my often-solitary travels and, I hope, enliven what would otherwise be a rather barren narrative.

# # #

Silver Bay, Minnesota: The Cost of Clean Water

When it was calm, and the sun shone bright, I could sit in my canoe, where the depth was upwards of six fathoms, and plainly see huge piles of stone at the bottom, of different shapes, some of which appeared as if they were hewn. The water at this time was as pure and transparent as air; and my canoe seemed as if it hung suspended in that element. It was impossible to look attentively through this limpid medium at the rocks below, without finding, before many minutes were elapsed, your head swim, and your eye no longer able to behold the dazzling scene.

> Jonathan Carver, *Travels Through the Interior Parts of North America in the Years 1766, 1767, and 1768* (describing his canoe trip along the North Shore of Lake Superior in 1767)

Today Minnesota Route 61 follows the rugged North Shore of Lake Superior for 150 miles from Duluth, Minnesota, to the Canadian border near Thunder Bay, Ontario. Within the city limits of Duluth the highway is a busy, predominantly residential thoroughfare named London Road. London Road has long been a preferred local address, and as one drives northeast out of the city, its lakeside presents an impressive row of mansions and substantial homes built in the early twentieth century by the area's iron and timber barons and inhabited today by many of its civic and business leaders. On a smaller scale this part of Duluth is reminiscent of Chicago's affluent North Shore suburbs, and like those imposing, venerable communities, London Road and its houses speak of a different era, one of gentility and force, propriety and stigma, privilege and oppression.

At city's edge the road forks: Minnesota Route 61, a modern expressway, veers slightly inland, while Saint Louis County Route 61—the original two-laned highway, now known as the Scenic Drive—hugs the lakeshore for fifteen miles before the two routes converge again near the town of Two Harbors. Originally a small Scandinavian settlement, Two Harbors received its first impetus for growth in 1884, when the Duluth and Iron Range Railroad was completed from Tower, Minnesota, and the town became a major shipping point for the high-grade iron ore mined in the Mesabi and Vermilion Ranges. At one time the largest iron-ore loading dock in the world was located here, and the 3M Company was born in a modest building on the corner of Waterfront Drive and Second Avenue. Like many towns around the lake, however, Two Harbors today seems on the verge of a new era. Although still one of the busiest harbors on Lake Superior, the town is in the process of transforming itself (or of being transformed) into a tourist destination. In recent years motels, restaurants, and gift shops have proliferated, and on summer and fall weekends traffic through town slows to a crawl.

Two Harbors marks a frontier of sorts. After negotiating its bustle, one enters a quieter, more pristine world, one on which the human grip perceptibly weakens. The old highway again finds the lakeshore, tight-roping along wave-battered cliffs, skirting rocky promontories, and sweeping around pebbled coves. To the northwest forested slopes rise to a serrated ridgeline, and myriad streams and rivers cascade toward the lake from the higher country. Along the highway are signs of human use and occupation—driveways to rustic cabins and lakeside resorts, occasional gas stations and stores catering to the tourist trade—but the dominant effect is of being on the edge of a vast and ancient wilderness. The rock is dark and volcanic, and the land is cloaked by a dense, variegated forest—the southern edge of the boreal forest—dominated by somber stands of balsam fir and black and white spruce, lightened here by glades of aspen and birch and pockets of maple, oak, and ash. Compared with much of the United States today, this part of Minnesota supports an atavistic abundance of wildlife—moose, black bears, and timber wolves; lynx and snowshoe hares.

Always delimiting the forested landscape, however, and contrasting dramatically with it, is the lake. Whereas the forest is an intricate mosaic of trees and undergrowth, the lake is a study in space and austerity. Like the ocean, its expansive surface reflects and concentrates the atmosphere. On clear, calm days its surface is a pacific mirror of the sky; on stormy ones a graphite cauldron of chop and swell. On this bright, breezy September morning the lake's faceted surface glitters like a sapphire plain. For thirty miles out of Duluth its southern shore is visible as a smoky smudge on the horizon; but as the lake widens, the opposite shore disappears below the earth's curve and the view to the southeast is of a pure, aqueous world, a world of water and sky, of wave and cloud—immense, impassive, seemingly immune to human influence.

* * *

The Silver Bay taconite-beneficiating and iron-ore-shipping facility of Northshore Mining straddles Route 61 on the outskirts of Silver Bay, a bustling company town located about fifty miles northeast of Duluth. The facility is quintessentially industrial, consisting of enormous corrugated metal buildings, massive cranes on steel superstructures, concrete storage silos, and smoke stacks emitting billows of steam. Half a mile up the highway the company's offices occupy a flat-roofed, two-story building of 1950s vintage whose plain, beige exterior, displaying rows of dark, rectangular windows, resembles an old computer punch card.

Several weeks ago I called to arrange for a tour of the facility, a common request for which Northshore has assigned responsibility to one of its longtime managers. But he has been called away on a family emergency, and my guide today is Wayne Johnson, a plant foreman. Wayne is a trim, energetic man in his midfifties, with gray hair, a matching mustache, and silver, wire-rimmed bifocals. Dressed neatly in faded gray jeans, a long-sleeved, light-blue work shirt, and well-used (but well-cared-for) work boots, he has a dapper air. I can almost imagine him sitting behind a desk in a bank in a pinstriped suit, a pipe stem emerging from his breast pocket. During our introduction I learn that he grew up in a small town in southern Minnesota—with an accent to prove it—and has worked for Northshore for eight years. His manner tends to the avuncular, and as we stand in the office getting acquainted, he jokes good-naturedly with me, with the pretty young receptionist, and with coworkers who stop by the office on company business. When I say, in response to his question, that I would like to tour the entire facility for an article I am researching, I can see him mentally writing off his morning. But he gamely tries to hide his disappointment.

"Sounds like you want the twenty-five-cent tour, not the nickel tour," he says. "No sir, not the nickel tour."

After outfitting me with the required hard hat, Wayne drives us in one of Northshore's battered company pickup trucks to the railcar-unloading building, the first stop on our tour and the terminus of a forty-seven-mile-long rail line from the company's taconite mine in Babbitt, Minnesota. Taconite, Wayne explains, is raw rock containing 20-30 percent iron. At the mine it is blasted out of the earth, crushed to pieces about four inches in diameter, and loaded into railroad cars for transport to Silver Bay. Each car carries eighty-seven "long tons" of taconite—a long ton equals 2,240 pounds—and each train consists of 120-160 cars pulled by four diesel locomotives. The railcar-unloading building at Silver Bay is located on a hillside above the rest of the plant. After the trains arrive at the site, the locomotives pull slowly through this building, stopping repeatedly to allow two cars at a time to dump their contents into enormous hoppers that gravity-feed the rock to the "crusher building" located downhill.

The crusher building is exactly what its name indicates: a place where "cone crushers"—giant steel drums—break and grind the rock into pieces of taconite about three-quarters of an inch in diameter. The "three-quarter-inch taconite" is then conveyed through a conduit under the highway to the enormous corrugated metal buildings along the lakeshore for further processing.

Our tour continues in these buildings, where "dry cobbers" magnetically separate rock that contains an acceptable percentage of iron from inferior rock, which becomes coarse, dry waste. The acceptable rock is then milled by steel rods and balls, hydro-separated, magnetically separated (again), and treated with acetic acid to produce an enriched concentrate that is more than 60 percent iron. This part of the process creates a slurry of tailings that is temporarily stored in nearby ponds for later permanent disposal. Finally, the iron concentrate is "pelletized" by mixing it with adhesive bentonite, tumbling the mixture in giant drums to form globular pellets, and firing and hardening the pellets at 2400°F. The end product, emerging on a conveyer system from a linear blast furnace whose dark interior glows orange with flame, is millions of pellets the size and density of small marbles, pellets that are easier to ship than the amorphous concentrate.

The building where the milling and enrichment occur, nondescript from the outside, is impressive inside—vast, cavernous, and illuminated only dimly by electric lights suspended from the high ceiling. A sprawling system of massive (even monstrous) machines occupies the ground level, and a network of steel ladders and catwalks provides elevated passage above the labyrinth. When the facility is operating (as it is during our tour), a deafening white noise fills the building, and a fine dust, smelling faintly like gunpowder, swirls through the air. Everywhere is dangerous motion—armatures turning, drums rotating, pulleys spinning, conveyer belts running—and a slurry of tailings flows in an open conduit, past vats of noxious chemicals. The whole scene is Stygian, infernal. The Silver Bay facility was constructed in 1955, but this building seems a relic of an earlier era. This is a latter-day example of the brute heavy industry that was the hallmark of the Industrial Revolution.

Appearances notwithstanding, the Silver Bay facility has been modernized several times since it was constructed and now employs industry-leading technology. Wayne shows me the control room, a dark, temperature-regulated, soundproofed room located on one of the milling/enrichment building's upper levels, where two men monitor a series of computers that control some of the crucial steps in the beneficiating process. Those computers control, for example, the strength of the electromagnets that separate iron-bearing particles of milled taconite from "barren" particles, thereby determining the composition of the final concentrate.

Wayne has apparently received some training in public relations and interpretive technique, for he occasionally stops and poses a question for me to answer or ponder. He does so with a gleam in his eyes that could be playful or malicious or both.

"How much do you think this cone crusher cost?" he asks early in the tour, chuckling when I underestimate the number by a factor of five.

At other times during the tour he leans toward me and whispers in a confidential, almost conspiratorial tone, as if he is going to disclose a trade secret or reveal some negative information about his employer. When he does so, he always prefaces his remarks by saying, "Now don't quote me on this, . . ." or "Now I wouldn't want you to write any of this down, . . ." But every fact he conveys is clearly for public consumption, and every comment he makes about Northshore is unfailingly complimentary. The Silver Bay facility cost hundreds of millions of dollars and meets all environmental standards. Northshore is not a union shop but treats its employees well, and benefits are generous. The facility's payroll supports the local economy. Wayne is a good company man.

We emerge from the control room to inspect the nearby "clarifying ponds," where the tailings slurry from the milling and enrichment process is temporarily impounded before being pumped seven miles over a 675-foot-high inland ridge to the permanent disposal area known as "Milepost 7." The ponds contain water with an unnatural color and sheen, and they are fenced and signed for safety. Farther along the shore is the company's massive coal-fired power plant, which produces all the electricity necessary to operate the facility and energize the town of Silver Bay. Our tour of the lakeshore facility concludes with the company's loading dock, where taconite pellets are stored in giant silos and loaded by conveyer belts onto thousand-foot-long ore ships for transport to various steelmakers along the lower Great Lakes for use in the manufacture of automobiles, appliances, tools, and toys.

Northshore is owned by Cliffs Minnesota Minerals Company, a wholly owned subsidiary of Cleveland Cliffs, Inc., the largest producer of iron pellets in the world. Cleveland Cliffs acquired the Silver Bay facility in 1994 from Cypress Minerals Company, which, in turn, had acquired it in 1986 from Reserve Mining Company, as Reserve was spiraling into bankruptcy. Today the facility employs about five hundred people and produces about 4.2 million tons of iron pellets per year. During Reserve's ownership the facility employed as many as three thousand people and production reached a high of almost eleven million tons per year. That was "before industry economic conditions forced its closure," as Northshore's public-relations brochure blandly puts it. That economic downturn followed a momentous lawsuit filed by the United States government against Reserve in 1972 and prosecuted over the next five years by the United States Department of Justice and Environmental Protection Agency. That "environmental trial," as Wayne refers to it during the tour, helped drive Reserve into bankruptcy and caused enormous social turmoil in this part of Minnesota.

* * *

In 1947, motivated by a robust economy, recently enacted tax laws favorable to the taconite industry, and the depletion of naturally occurring high-grade iron ore in the Mesabi Range, Reserve Mining Company announced plans to construct a taconite-beneficiating facility on the North Shore of Lake Superior. The company applied to the State of Minnesota for the necessary permits, including one from the state's Water Pollution Control Commission to discharge tailings into the lake. In its applications Reserve posited that the tailings, heavier than water, would form a "density current" that would flow to the bottom of the lake. The coarser tailings would settle first, forming a near-shore delta, while the finer tailings would drift farther offshore, finally settling in the lake's "great trough," where they would lie harmless and undisturbed through the eons. After a series of public hearings at which the only substantial opposition came from a group of sport fishermen, the permits were issued in December 1947.

Four years later Reserve began to construct its lakeshore beneficiating facility and the nearby town of Silver Bay. The completed facility shipped its first load of enriched iron-ore pellets in April 1956. By the late 1960s, after several plant expansions, Reserve was discharging 67,000 tons of tailings per day into Lake Superior. Although the ratio was vehemently disputed during the later litigation, in terms of suspended solids those tailings probably exceeded by a factor of five or six the amount of suspended solids entering the lake from all natural sources combined. By some estimates Reserve's discharges into the lake were the largest industrial discharges in the world. The exhaust stacks of Reserve's facility were also emitting large amounts of steam and by-product into the air at Silver Bay. In short, by the late 1960s Reserve was arguably the world's largest polluter.

Unfortunately for Reserve, the construction and expansion of its Silver Bay facility coincided with the rise of the modern environmental movement. The Clean Water Act, originally enacted in 1948 as the Federal Water Pollution Control Act, was amended and significantly strengthened during the 1960s and early 1970s. On January 1, 1970, President Richard M. Nixon signed into law the National Environmental Policy Act of 1969, and in December 1970 supported the creation of the Environmental Protection Agency through a reorganization of the executive branch; for the first time in history a single federal agency was delegated primary authority to enforce the nation's major environmental laws. Numerous other federal and state laws reflected the nation's increasing awareness of, and concern about, environmental degradation. Those legal and political developments reflected a change in societal values of which Reserve seemed almost willfully ignorant. The company did nothing to ameliorate the growing public concern about the highly visible effects of its discharges into Lake Superior: miles-long plumes of cloudy green water (a distinct contrast to the lake's naturally clear, ultramarine water);

reduced fish catches; gray slime growing on fishing nets. The company, the most potent economic force in northeastern Minnesota and a generous contributor to the reelection campaigns of John Blatnik, the local congressman, apparently believed it was immune to any serious criticism or effective enforcement action.

The 1960s also marked a time of increased awareness of, and research into, the deleterious health effects of various industrial agents and by-products. The taconite mined by Reserve near Babbitt contains large percentages of minerals known as amphibole silicates, including two closely related minerals named cummingtonite and grunerite. The tailings produced by Reserve's beneficiation process likewise contain large amounts of pulverized cummingtonite and grunerite. Cummingtonite and grunerite are similar in chemical composition to amosite asbestos. During the 1947 permit hearings the City of Duluth's public health officer had expressed concern about the effect of Reserve's tailings on Duluth's municipal water supply, which was drawn directly from the lake, but his concern had been brushed aside in the general enthusiasm for the new project.

Exposure to asbestos had long been linked to various health problems, and a 1960 South African study had reported a correlation between asbestos exposure and mesothelioma, a particularly lethal cancer of the pleura or peritoneum. Then, in 1964, three American physicians—one of them a prominent doctor at the Mount Sinai School of Medicine named Irving J. Selikoff—published a study of the health problems associated with occupational asbestos exposure. That study found a significantly elevated incidence of lung cancer, cancer of the gastrointestinal tract, and mesothelioma among workers exposed to asbestos over a twenty-year period. By 1973 the federal government had recommended the adoption of an occupational standard for asbestos exposure. But there was no scientific consensus on the threshold level of exposure posing a significant threat to human health or on whether ingestion of asbestos fibers, as opposed to inhalation, was correlated with the identified cancers.

Although the controversy over Reserve's discharges into Lake Superior initially arose out of public concerns about impacts to the lake's aesthetic values and its commercial and sport fisheries, it quickly evolved to include concerns about the potential public health issues, which significantly elevated the matter's profile. In January 1968 the United States Department of the Interior formed a multi-agency Taconite Study Group whose summary report, produced later that year, concluded that Reserve's tailings were in fact polluting the lake. That report prompted Secretary of the Interior Stewart L. Udall to announce in January 1969, only days before he left office, that, under the provisions of the Clean Water Act and as a prelude to possible legal action, he was convening a formal enforcement conference for Lake Superior. The purpose of the conference was to determine whether pollution originating in one state was endangering the health or welfare of persons in another—a prerequisite to federal jurisdiction under the act—and, if so, to try to negotiate a resolution to the matter.

The Conference in the Matter of Pollution of the Interstate Waters of Lake Superior and its Tributary Basin convened in Duluth on May 13, 1969. The conferees quickly focused their attention on Reserve's discharges. (Significantly, government scientists, using cummingtonite as a tracer, had recently detected the presence of Reserve's tailings in the public water supplies of Duluth, Two Harbors, and Beaver Bay, Minnesota.) The atmosphere during the three-day conference was adversarial. Through presentations by its company officers and engineers and a team of expert consultants Reserve vigorously contested the findings and conclusions in the study group's summary report and vehemently disputed the economic and technological feasibility of alternative on-land disposal sites. Not surprisingly, the conference adjourned without the conferees reaching any consensus.

Between May 1969 and January 1971 the enforcement conference convened four more times without significant progress. Government scientists presented evidence that Reserve's tailings were present in the waters of the State of Wisconsin, satisfying the requirement for federal jurisdiction, and the conferees (as well as the public) increasingly focused their attention on the presence of the tailings in the public water supplies of the various communities. In response, Reserve seemed content to stonewall on the factual issues and to present evidence of alleged conflicts-of-interest by the participating state officials.

Finally, on April 23, 1971, the conference chairman signaled its end by reading into the record the following statement:

> I can only conclude that the time for direct and immediate Federal action is at hand. In the event that the Administrator of the Environmental Protection Agency adopts the course of action which I will recommend to him, the Reserve Mining Company will be required to propose a plan for pollution abatement which is acceptable

to the United States Environmental Protection Agency within 180 days or be subject to a suit by the United States.

After more than two years of fruitless negotiations, federal legal action against Reserve appeared imminent.

* * *

Within President Nixon's administration, it is safe to say, the idea of suing a major industrial entity like Reserve caused considerable concern. Reserve and its parent companies were generous contributors to Republican candidates and campaigns, but Nixon himself had recognized the growing political power of the environmental movement by campaigning as an "environmental candidate" in 1968 and by supporting several strong environmental initiatives, including the creation of the Environmental Protection Agency. He had appointed as the first administrator of the EPA an apparently lackluster, unsuccessful Republican senatorial candidate from Indiana named William Ruckelshaus. Ruckelshaus, however, took his new job seriously and, navigating the dangerous waters of the administration, sought approval to take action against Reserve. On January 19, 1972, after receiving the go-ahead from John Ehrlichman, one of Nixon's senior White House advisors, Ruckelshaus sent a letter to Attorney General John Mitchell formally requesting that the Department of Justice file an enforcement action against Reserve.

A month later the United States filed its complaint in the United States District Court for the District of Minnesota, initiating the lawsuit known as *United States of America v.*

Reserve Mining Company. The federal government alleged, among other things, that Reserve's discharges of amphibole fibers into the water of Lake Superior violated the water quality standards promulgated by the State of Minnesota under the Clean Water Act and that its discharges into the lake and air constituted common law nuisances. The government sought an injunction against Reserve to abate the pollution. Other parties—including the States of Wisconsin and Michigan, the cities of Duluth and Superior, Wisconsin, and several environmental organizations—intervened as plaintiffs, aligning themselves with the federal government, while Saint Louis and Lake Counties, several nearby towns, and several business organizations intervened as defendants, aligning themselves with Reserve. The State of Minnesota declined to intervene but about six months later, on Reserve's motion, was involuntarily joined as a plaintiff. (Reserve's motive was to bind the state to the federal court's decision, which it apparently believed would be in its favor.) By the start of trial more than twenty parties were involved in the litigation.

The case was assigned to Judge Miles Welton Lord, at that time already a well-known figure in Minnesota politics. Born in 1919 into a large working-class family in Crosby, Minnesota, in the Cuyuna Iron Range—his father a lumberjack, his mother a Sunday school teacher—Judge Lord was proud of his blue-collar roots. He had worked his way through college and law school at the University of Minnesota as a welder, janitor, logger, and ditch-digger. As a child, growing up in tough, heavily ethnic neighborhoods, he had also learned how to fight, and at the age of nineteen had boxed in the Golden Gloves Upper Midwest Regional Championship. (He liked to boast about how, in the championship bout, he had been knocked down seventeen times but had finished on his feet.) His pugnacity and persistence served him well in the political arena. He rose to prominence in the state's Democratic-Farmer-Labor Party; served three terms as the state's Attorney General; and in 1961, under Senator Hubert Humphrey's sponsorship, was appointed United States Attorney for the District of Minnesota. Then, in 1966, President Lyndon B. Johnson nominated him to the federal bench.

Not surprisingly, Judge Lord's early life seems to have instilled in him two enduring characteristics: sympathy for society's have-nots, and a conviction that rules should be applied even-handedly. Initially at least, those characteristics inclined him to be sympathetic to Reserve and its workers. At a pretrial conference on April 10, 1972, he revealed that during the Great Depression his family had dumped tailings into a lake near Crosby. He also assured Reserve's supporters that Reserve was not going "to be forced to close their operation. I don't think anything I do here will cost them one job. . . . When the labor union leaders came to me and suggested that this proceeding might put them out of jobs, I said I didn't think it was possible under the law to do that." Judge Lord's background and comments concerned the government's attorneys, who discussed the possibility of filing a motion to disqualify him. In the end, however, they decided that he was "as good as they were likely to get."

The trial, which began on August 1, 1973, lasted 139 days. More than a hundred witnesses testified, and more than sixteen hundred exhibits were introduced into evidence. The transcript of the proceedings ran to more than eighteen thousand pages. Despite his pre-trial comments, Judge Lord proved to have an open, inquisitive mind, and during the trial he focused his attention on three interrelated issues: whether Reserve's tailings and emissions were the source of the amphibole fibers found in Lake Superior's waters, including in the drinking water supplies of Duluth and Superior, Wisconsin, and in the ambient air at Silver Bay; whether ingestion or inhalation of those fibers posed a risk to public health; and whether there were feasible alternatives to Reserve's disposal of its tailings in Lake Superior. On the first issue, the government presented compelling mineralogical and limnological evidence, only ineffectively rebutted by Reserve, that Reserve's tailings and emissions were the source of the amphibole fibers. On the second issue, in the absence of authoritative epidemiological studies, the government attempted, through a series of expert witnesses, to build a circumstantial case showing that ingestion of amphibole fibers posed a significant threat to public health. The government's culminating witness was Dr. Selikoff, who testified forcefully that in his opinion it was "highly probable" that ingestion of amphibole fibers, as in drinking water drawn from Lake Superior, would eventually cause an increase in gastrointestinal cancers. He also testified that inhalation of amphibole fibers in the concentrations reported in the air of Silver Bay would probably result in more deaths. Then, in concluding his direct testimony, he said somewhat carelessly, "I think we ought to have a sign at the entrance of . . . the town [of Silver Bay], 'Please Close Your Windows Before Driving Through.' I certainly would want to close mine." The next day, however, alarmed by the media's sensational coverage of his statements, Dr. Selikoff "clarified" his testimony in a way that was widely perceived as his recanting critical portions of it.

On the third issue, the government argued that on-land disposal of tailings, either near Reserve's mine at Babbitt, Minnesota, or near its beneficiating facility at Silver Bay, was both economically and technologically feasible. Reserve opposed all such proposals, asserting, for example, that moving the facility to Babbitt was technologically infeasible because of an inadequate water supply and that, in any event, it would cost the company almost $400 million to do so. Reserve adamantly maintained that a proposal known as the "deep pipe plan" was the only feasible alternative. Under that plan Reserve would continue to discharge its tailings into Lake Superior, but the tailings first would be "flocculated"—bound together into small clumps through the addition of organic compounds—and then discharged through a pipeline extending into the lake to a depth of 150 feet. A "density current" would carry the flocculated tailings to a depth of 600 feet, where they would slowly accumulate, in situ, on the lakebed. According to Reserve, the deep pipe plan would safeguard the lake; it would also cost the company substantially less than any on-land disposal.

Despite Dr. Selikoff's "clarification" of his testimony, the evidence presented by the government had impressed Judge Lord with the seriousness of the threat to public health posed by Reserve's discharges and emissions. On February 5, 1974, to encourage Reserve to enter into serious settlement negotiations, the judge took the unusual step of announcing to the parties that in his view the government had made a *prima facie* case of a threat to public health. Based on his comments the judge clearly wanted Reserve to consider some form of on-land disposal of tailings that would eliminate all discharges into Lake Superior. Reserve, however, obstinately refused to consider any such proposal, maintaining that all were economically and technologically infeasible.

During this time Judge Lord apparently began to suspect that Reserve was not acting in good faith. On March 1, in response to a subpoena requested by the government but suggested indirectly (and quite improperly) by the judge himself, Reserve's parent corporations, Armco Steel and Republic Steel, produced hundreds of previously undisclosed documents. One of those documents was an internal memorandum stating that it was "technically feasible" to dispose of tailings at the Babbitt site. Another was a 1972 report of an engineering task force questioning the feasibility of the deep pipe plan and recommending that the company not "pursu[e] this concept any further." Many of the documents discussed a plan to dispose of tailings on land at a site known as Palisade Creek, near Silver Bay.

Judge Lord was irate, and he directed his wrath at the corporate officers present in court. The next day Reserve informed the judge that the asserted technical problems with on-land disposal had suddenly been resolved and that they were ready to discuss a negotiated settlement. Judge Lord ordered Reserve to prepare a cost estimate for building an on-land disposal facility near Silver Bay. The company responded with a "concept" and a cost estimate of $574.5 million that Judge Lord characterized as a "cruel hoax" and "outrageously inflated." He had had enough. On April 20 he released a brief memorandum opinion (followed three weeks later by a 109-page-long typewritten "supplemental opinion") announcing his decision on the merits of the case. In his opinion Judge Lord found that the taconite tailings contained large quantities of minute amphibole fibers that are morphologically and chemically identical or similar to amosite asbestos. He further found that:

6) Exposure to these fibers can produce asbestosis, mesothelioma, and cancer of the lung, gastrointestinal tract and larynx . . .

9) The discharge into the air substantially endangers the health of the people of Silver Bay and surrounding communities as far away as the eastern shore [of Lake Superior] in Wisconsin.

10) The discharge into the water substantially endangers the health of the people who procure their drinking water from the western arm of Lake Superior, including the communities of Beaver Bay, Two Harbors, Cloquet, Duluth, and Superior, Wisconsin . . .

12) The exposure of a non-worker populace cannot be equated with industrial exposure if for no other reason than the environmental exposure, as contrasted to a working exposure, is for every hour of every day.

Judge Lord then enjoined all discharges into Lake Superior as of 12:01 a.m. the next morning, April 21, 1974.

The companies immediately appealed the injunction to the Eighth Circuit Court of Appeals, where, on June 4, 1974, a conservative panel of the court issued its initial decision in the case. The court first stated, "Of course, foremost consideration must be given to any demonstrable danger to the public health." It then made explicit what was implicit in that apparently innocuous bromide: that absent such *demonstrable* danger, "the public interest may arguably be served either way in environmental matters." The court then critically reviewed the medical evidence received by the trial court, particularly the testimony of Dr. Selikoff and Dr. Arnold Brown, an impartial expert appointed by Judge Lord to assist him in understanding the health issues. Unlike Judge Lord, however, the court of appeals found the medical evidence to be inconclusive. Given that uncertainty and in light of the enormous personal, social, and economic impacts of a long-term plant closure, the court declined to keep the facility closed. Accordingly, it granted a stay of Judge Lord's injunction conditioned "upon Reserve taking prompt steps to abate its discharges into the air and water." (The plaintiffs immediately applied to the United States Supreme Court for an order vacating or modifying the court of appeals' order. On October 11, 1974, the Supreme Court, over the scathing dissent of Justice William O. Douglas, denied the application.)

On remand to the district court Reserve proffered anew its Palisade Creek disposal plan, which the plaintiffs opposed on the ground that it would degrade a unique and scenic natural area. After a twelve-day hearing Judge Lord recommended rejection of the plan. In doing so, he chided Reserve for intentionally distorting the legal significance of the court of appeals' decision; for acting in bad faith throughout the litigation; and, with respect to the plan itself, for playing a "corporate shell game" and presenting a plan that was at best conceptual. He questioned the engineering feasibility of Reserve's plan and emphatically denied its "ecological reasonableness." He waxed poetic, describing his own visit to the area and quoting the renowned environmentalist Sigurd Olson, before concluding:

> The Court cannot view the ecology with their
> [Reserve's witnesses'] "tunnel vision." The

Palisades area provides a place upon which to roam, to be free, to enjoy the opulence of the scenic wonders that have been provided by nature. This Court cannot allow the present greed of a few to deny a priceless treasure to many. It cannot allow the immediate problems of some to cheat others of their environmental birthright.

By late 1974 the case was again before the Eighth Circuit, which consolidated seven different appeals filed by the various parties to the litigation. On March 14, 1975, the court issued its own lengthy decision on the merits. After reviewing the evidence proffered to the district court, the court predictably resumed its previous course of compromise. The court observed that Congress had "generally geared its national environmental policy to allowing polluting industries a reasonable period of time to make adjustments in their efforts to conform to federal standards." Finding that the district court had "abused its discretion by immediately closing this major industrial plant," the court concluded that "Reserve must be given a reasonable opportunity and a reasonable time to construct facilities to accomplish an abatement of its pollution of air and water and the health risk created thereby. In this way, hardship to employees and great economic loss incident to an immediate plant closure may be avoided." The court suggested that one year was a reasonable amount of time for Reserve to obtain the necessary permits from the State of Minnesota for on-land disposal of its tailings.

The day following the court of appeals' decision Judge Lord convened a hearing at which he directed the relevant state agencies to establish a timetable for the permit proceedings and publicly encouraged the state's legislature and governor to take a more active role in resolving the dispute. The court of appeals, learning of the hearing through news reports, obtained and reviewed a transcript of it. In a supplemental opinion released on April 8, 1975, the court characterized the hearing as "irregular" and chastised Judge Lord for what it perceived as his attempts to influence the forthcoming state permit proceedings.

Judge Lord, frustrated by Reserve's continuing resistance to serious settlement discussions and, perhaps, by the court of appeals' heavy-handed involvement in what was, after all, his case, acted in an increasingly belligerent manner toward Reserve. In November 1975 he convened an unusual "educational hearing" to discuss the provision of safe drinking water to the City of Duluth and to which he directed a United States Marshall to summon state and local officials. At the conclusion of that hearing he ordered Reserve to deliver to the city a $100,000 check to pay for the costs of providing temporary water filtration. He then intemperately added, "And there will be no stay on that. That is a firm and final order. That may be appealed, but I do not certify it for appeal because I am not at all in doubt about its propriety."

Reserve, of course, immediately appealed the order to the Eighth Circuit. In December 1975 Judge Lord, sensing the seriousness of the situation, appeared personally before the court of appeals to defend his actions, but to no avail. On January 6, 1976, the court issued an extraordinary (perhaps unprecedented) written opinion censuring him for his handling of the case:

> The record demonstrates overt acts by the district judge reflecting great bias against Reserve

Mining Company and substantial disregard for the mandate of this court. . . .

Judge Lord seems to have shed the robe of the judge and to have assumed the mantle of the advocate. The court thus becomes lawyer, witness and judge in the same proceeding, and abandons the greatest virtue of a fair and conscientious judge—impartiality. . . .

Disregard of this court's mandate by a lawyer would be contemptuous; it can hardly be excused when the reckless action emanates from a judicial officer. It is one thing for a district judge to disagree on a legal basis with a judgment of this court. It is quite another to openly challenge the court's ruling and attempt to discredit the integrity of the judgment in the eyes of the public. . . .

Our system of government is premised upon subservience to the rule of law. If a judge in the exercise of judicial power loses sight of these principles, the result is autocratic rule by lawless judicial action.

On its own motion the court then removed Judge Lord from the case and directed the Chief Judge of the District of Minnesota to assign it to a new trial judge.

Reserve installed scrubbers on its stacks. After extended litigation in the state judicial system the Minnesota Supreme Court ordered the state agencies to issue the permits necessary for the company to construct a permanent, on-land tailings-disposal facility at the alternative site known as Milepost 7. The facility was designed to accommodate all the tailings that would be produced during the estimated life of the Babbitt mine—forty years—and the permits required Reserve to maintain the disposal site in a safe condition in perpetuity. The federal-court litigation finally concluded, under the supervision of Chief Judge Edward J. Devitt, in the spring of 1977. (Among other things, Judge Devitt fined Reserve $837,500 for violating its previously-issued state permits and $200,000 for violating various court rules and orders.) Working against a court-ordered deadline, Reserve completed construction of the Milepost 7 disposal facility in the spring of 1980. The installation of the scrubbers and the construction of the disposal facility, which at times required 2,800 workers, cost approximately $370 million.

Unfortunately for Reserve, its timing was again bad: the early 1980s saw a dramatic decline in the demand for domestic steel. By 1982 the company was laying off workers, and in 1986, after declaring bankruptcy, it closed its Silver Bay facility. The facility sat idle for three years before Cyprus Minerals purchased it for $680 million. Four years later Cyprus sold it to Cleveland Cliffs. Between 1980 and 1990 Silver Bay's population had declined from 2,917 to 1,894; by 2000, after a decade of increased efficiency and diminished expectations, it had rebounded slightly to 2,068.

Judge Lord, who eventually served as chief judge of the district court, continued to hear controversial cases, including one in which he upheld the constitutionality of the legislation establishing the Boundary Waters Canoe Area Wilderness in Superior National Forest and another in which he held that federal regulations permitting the hunting of timber wolves in Minnesota were illegal. In 1985, after receiving another stern reprimand from the Eight Circuit for his handling of another case, he retired from the federal bench and went into private practice with his son in the Twin Cities area, where, for the rest of his life, he represented plaintiffs in personal-injury actions.

* * *

Now, forty-five years after the litigation's conclusion, it is possible, perhaps, to view the Reserve controversy with some dispassion. Knowing what we now know about ecosystem function, Reserve's assertions that its discharges into Lake Superior were benign seem at best fatuous and at worst fraudulent. But if we return to the beginning of the story, to the 1940s, when Reserve announced its proposal to construct the Silver Bay facility and applied for the necessary state permits, I question whether Reserve should be made to bear the entire burden of fault. After all, the modern science of ecology has only confirmed a basic truth that people have known for hundreds or even thousands of years: that one cannot alter one component of an integrated system without altering the entire system. Even in the 1940s people knew, or should have known, that Reserve's assurances about its discharges into Lake Superior were too good to be true. Promising industry without pollution, prosperity without cost, cause without effect, Reserve told the people of the North Shore (and Minnesota as a whole) what they wanted to hear, and the people eagerly accepted it. Like smokers who choose to ignore the fact that their habit is responsible for the deaths of hundreds of thousands of their fellow smokers every year, the people chose to ignore what, at some level, they knew to be true.

But it was also inevitable, knowing what we now know about the rise of the modern environmental movement, that

Reserve would eventually be forced to cease its discharges into Lake Superior. So, looking back, one cannot help but speculate on Reserve's corporate motives (to the extent that it is fair to assign motives to a complex, inanimate organization) in refusing to compromise to bring an early end to the controversy and conflict. Reserve's intransigence through years of negotiation and litigation is indeed puzzling. One possible explanation, of course, is that Reserve was just another large, arrogant American corporation—secure in its power, dismissive of those who opposed it, and unwilling to change its highly profitable mode of operation to address what it viewed as overwrought concerns about public health and environmental degradation.

On the other hand, perhaps even then Reserve knew that the outcome was inevitable, and perhaps the posture it adopted in negotiation and litigation was the result of a cynical (even Machiavellian) corporate strategy. By utilizing uncompromising, bare-knuckled (and arguably dilatory) tactics, Reserve was able to extend its Silver Bay operations for years beyond what might have been possible had it cooperated with government regulators and environmental organizations. The delay was enormously profitable for Reserve and its parent companies. One of the government attorneys who litigated the case against Reserve estimated that in 1970, for example, Reserve spent $700,000 on lawyers and consultants to defend itself but returned about $20 million in after-tax profits to its parent companies. For 1971 the numbers were $350,000 and $19 million; for 1972, $630,000 and $14.9 million.

In any event, from our vantage point today, the outcome of the Reserve controversy appears inevitable. The United States—a democratic nation more responsive than most to its citizens' concerns and the wealthiest, most technologically advanced nation in the history of the world, a nation that could afford to impose reasonable measures to protect its citizens' health, pacify their concerns, and preserve one of its most remarkable natural resources—was not going to allow the world's largest industrial polluter to continue to operate within its borders, especially not when public opinion turned and clearly favored the imposition of protective measures. Reserve may have been a large corporation, but it was only one of hundreds of large corporations doing business in the United States. A big fish but an even bigger pond. The only question, really, was how quickly Reserve would be made to abate its discharges.

Viewed in that light, Judge Lord's only mistake was that he cut to the chase. He had no patience with Reserve's admittedly vexing efforts to protect its corporate coffers, with the Eighth Circuit's reluctance to order a plant closure on the basis of less-than-certain scientific evidence, with the State of Minnesota's vacillations, with the public's waxing and waning interest in the case. He made up his mind, and he directed people to act. But just as the system wouldn't allow Reserve an unfettered hand, it wouldn't allow Judge Lord one. A judicial activist in the tradition of Justice William O. Douglas, whom he often cited as a role model, Judge Lord believed that the judiciary should lead the way. But in this case he got out too far ahead of the pack. And, like a tiring front-runner in a cross-country race, the pack reeled him in. Even today, when I ask my cousin, a lifelong Duluthian, about the litigation, he utters the one sentence that I fear will be Judge Lord's lasting impression on the public he sought to protect. "That judge," he says emphatically, "was crazy."

Did Reserve's discharges into Lake Superior pose a significant threat to public health and safety? Even today, after forty-five more years of research, the scientific evidence remains mixed as to whether the ingestion of amphibole fibers causes an elevated risk of gastrointestinal or other cancers. All one can say with certainty is that if the risk is elevated, it is far less than the risk of mesothelioma and other cancers associated with occupational exposure to airborne asbestos.

* * *

After we conclude our tour of the lakeshore facility, Wayne asks, somewhat reluctantly, if I would like to see the Milepost 7 disposal area. After I say yes, we again climb into the company's truck and drive on a rough, rocky service road that follows two parallel pipelines—one operational, one backup—away from the lake and diagonally up the ridge behind the railcar-unloading building. The pipelines, pressurized to 130 pounds per square inch, carry the slurry of tailings from the lakeshore clarifying ponds over the 675-foot-high ridge to the permanent disposal area at Milepost 7. Partway up the ridge we stop at a building where Wayne quickly inspects an intermediate pump. We then continue climbing through a young, open forest of balsam fir, aspen, and birch. The views of the big lake behind us are panoramic, breathtaking.

It has been a cordial tour, but as we approach Milepost 7, a nonspecific tension envelops the truck's cab. Wayne says anxiously, "Gee, I wish we'd see a deer. I always see deer on this road." And when I don't respond, he says it again, and then again. His manner is distracted, his tone robotic. We finally crest the ridge, descend a short distance on the other side, stop at a pullout, and climb out of the truck. Standing near a shade ramada, still elevated several hundred feet above the disposal area, we look over a surreal scene. The immense, rectilinear settling ponds of Milepost 7 dwarf my expectations. Several thousand acres of flat water, impounded behind dirt-and-aggregate dams, stretch to the north, toward Superior National Forest and the forests and lakes of the Boundary Waters. The color of the water is startlingly unnatural, garish—one impoundment chalky white, another cloudy turquoise. Rivulets of gray water leak from the dams, meandering across small, barren deltas. From where we stand the impoundments resemble a mosaic of sterile fields. Below the dams, in an area denuded of vegetation, a bulldozer, working with ant-like persistence, pushes piles of dirt against a growing earthwork.

Northshore's public-relations brochure informs me that "[t]he nearly six-mile square milepost 7 tailings disposal area, which has become a haven for wildlife, is continually monitored for contaminants." In the brochure that statement is illustrated by a carefully composed photograph of a woman in a hard hat crouching among sedges and other vegetation on the shore of a lake and examining a flask of clear water. The settling ponds at Milepost 7 look nothing like the lake in the brochure. I don't know why I am surprised: the brochure is a lie. Milepost 7 is a vile, lifeless place.

"Wildlife loves this area," Wayne says wanly. "If we went down to the ponds, you could see little fish in the water." His voice trails off. Even Wayne doesn't have the heart to continue. We stand together and stare silently at the desolation.

As we begin to drive back toward the lakeshore facility, I ponder the environmental compromise that produced Milepost 7. To save the world's largest and purest freshwater lake from further degradation, we, as a society, acting through our legal and political system, decided to sacrifice several thousand acres of lesser landscape, and to hide the destruction from public view behind a 675-foot-high ridge. Out of sight, out of mind. Forty-five years ago the alternative—the closure of the facility and the resulting economic and social dislocation—was unthinkable to too many people. And so, thanks to technological advances and capital investment, the good times eventually returned to Silver Bay. Some even believe that with additional technological advances the facility will be able to operate profitably indefinitely into the future.

But that view is, I think, naïvely optimistic or at least short-sighted, because the world will inevitably (and, I suspect, sooner rather than later) change: the taconite, like the richer ore before it, will be depleted; or the United States will decide that it no longer needs a domestic iron and steel industry (and will effectively export the jobs and environmental damage to less-developed nations); or technological advances will render the entire industry obsolete. Or, most hopefully (and unrealistically), we Americans, the world's ultimate consumers, may change our habits, may cease to demand the continuous and ever-changing supply of tantalizing manufactured products— the embarrassment of riches—that now characterizes our society and that requires and supports the industry of Silver Bay.

Indeed, as Wayne and I crest the ridge and the big lake again comes into view on this bright September morning, I find myself imagining a day not far off, as history is reckoned—a day perhaps only three or four decades in the future—when the gates have been locked, the equipment salvaged, and the railroad tracks abandoned; a day when aspens sprout along the chain-link fences, timber wolves lope across the highway, and the lake sends massive swells against the disintegrating dock—a day when the earth at last begins to reclaim its own.

# # #

Thunder Bay, Ontario: The Friction of Culture

1. We live longer: Canadians born today will live an average of three years longer than Americans (81 years in Canada versus 78.7 south of the border). Not only that, the gap between life expectancy in the two countries is widening with each passing decade—it was less than a year in the late 1970s.

2. We're more satisfied with our lives: According to the Better Life Index, an international quality of life comparison by the [Organisation for Economic Co-operation and Development] each year, Canadians enjoy a higher level of life satisfaction than Americans, scoring 7.4 out of 10, versus 7.0 in the U.S.

3. Saying "Sorry" is good for you: Canadians are mocked for always apologizing, but it's not a character flaw. Saying sorry has been found to boost happiness and strengthen relationships. Researchers at the University of Waterloo even found apologizing to a cop when pulled over for speeding can get fines reduced an average of $51. True, scientists did recently claim that refusing to apologize for your actions leads to a sense of empowerment, but such short-sighted thinking would only appeal to self-centred Americans. (Sorry, that was mean.)

Top three of "99 reasons why it's better to be Canadian," *Maclean's* (June 28, 2013)

Thunder Bay, Ontario, is a tough, energetic, working-class city of docks, shipyards, railroad tracks, grain elevators, lumber mills, ethnic neighborhoods, parks, rivers, and a small university. With a population of 125,000 it is the largest Canadian city between Toronto and Winnipeg—a northwesterly arc of more than a thousand miles—and edges out Duluth, Minnesota, as the largest city on the thirteen-hundred-mile circumference of Lake Superior. Because it functions as the retail and service center for most of northwestern Ontario, it feels bigger than its modest population suggests. A bustling provincial metropolis, it is the Canadian equivalent of, say, Omaha, Nebraska. On a big lake.

The modern city of Thunder Bay is an amalgamation of two former neighboring settlements, Port Arthur and Fort William, which consolidated in 1970. According to local folklore, a majority of citizens wanted to name their new city "Lakehead," but civic leaders so wanted to name the city after the expansive natural harbor that first attracted travelers and settlers here that they split the opposition by including both "Lakehead" and "The Lakehead" on the ballot. Whether or not that story is true, today "Thunder Bay" it is—a resonant, deep-throated name that seems to issue a challenge, like a bellowing moose, to people who venture to the wild, sparsely populated lake-and-forest country of northwestern Ontario.

The two settlements that constitute Thunder Bay have different histories and, even today, somewhat different identities. Fort William, now officially known as Thunder Bay South, traces its roots to a French fort established in 1717 near the mouth of the Kaministiquia River (locally known as the Kam). Then, in 1804, the North West Company relocated its most important fur-trading post from Grand Portage to the mouth of the Kam. The new post was called Fort William, after William McGillivray, one of the Scottish-owned company's prominent members. Its heyday was brief. After the North West Company merged with the Hudson's Bay Company in 1821, Fort William quickly declined in importance and entered a decades-long torpor from which it awoke only with the advent of large-scale shipping on Lake Superior in 1855, when the first locks were constructed at Sault Sainte Marie. It continued its resurgence in the twentieth century, when it was, for several decades, the largest shipper of grain from Canada's prairie provinces.

Port Arthur, now known as Thunder Bay North, got a later start. In 1870 General Garnet Wolseley landed at the eastern end of the Dawson Trail en route to Manitoba to suppress the Riel Rebellion and named the small settlement there Prince Arthur's Landing. In 1884, after the Canadian Pacific Railway was completed through the area, the growing town was incorporated as Port Arthur. With the railroad came railroad workers, including many Italians and Slavs. Finns immigrated to the area to work as lumberjacks and to fish commercially in Lake Superior, and also, perhaps, because the forested landscape and cold climate reminded them of home. And for most of the twentieth century the Port Arthur Shipbuilding Company was a major local employer, building dozens of large ships, including corvettes and minesweepers for the Royal Navy during World War II.

Today Thunder Bay is struggling to maintain or reinvent itself. Although the processing of forest products remains an important industry, in the 1980s Vancouver supplanted it as the premier grain-shipping port in Canada, and much of the shipbuilding industry long ago moved overseas. So in recent years Thunder Bay has looked to tourism to boost its sagging economy. And, to a surprising degree, it has succeeded. Outdoorsmen regularly stop in the city for a day or two before decamping for the Canadian bush, and the Ontario provincial government now operates, southwest of the city, an elaborate reconstruction of the original fur-trading post and living-history museum known as Old Fort William—a sort of Williamsburg of the North Woods. Although the two old downtowns are struggling, the newer city is coalescing around a retail shopping district and the campus of Lakehead University, located midway between the historic centers.

But Thunder Bay today is defined not so much by what it contains as by what contains it—the wilderness of the Canadian bush. Immediately east of the city, shielded from Lake Superior's storms and swells by the curving Sibley Peninsula— also known, more dramatically, as Thunder Cape—is the protected anchorage from which the modern city takes its name; immediately south of the city, looming more than a thousand feet above it and forming a natural barrier between Canada and the United States, are the Nor'Wester Mountains; and fifteen miles west, on the Kam, are Kakabeka Falls, touted as the "Niagara of the North." Beyond the city's reach to the north stretch the seemingly endless boreal forests and glaciated lakes of central Canada. The spirit of that invisible wilderness seems to permeate the city. Despite its modern amenities, Thunder Bay still feels like a frontier outpost, a jumping-off point, an edge of the modern, civilized world.

* * *

Driving from Duluth to Thunder Bay, one follows Minnesota Route 61 northeast for 150 miles along Lake Superior's rugged North Shore to the international boundary with Canada. (This part of Minnesota, knapped to a point by the lakeshore and the international boundary, has long been known as the Arrowhead because of its triangular shape.) Beyond the towns of Two Harbors, Silver Bay, and Grand Marais, one passes through the forested reservation of the Grand Portage Band of Lake Superior Chippewa Indians and the village of Grand Portage, with its dock for the Isle Royale ferries, and over the granitic shoulder of Mount Josephine to the international boundary, formed here by the chasmed torrent of the Pigeon River.

Although the United States and Canada are geographic neighbors and political allies and share similar histories and a common language, the international crossing gives one the first indication that things are going to be slightly different north of the border. At the crossing Canada Border Services Agency officers ask travelers a series of standard questions—What is your citizenship? What is the purpose of your visit? How long do you intend to stay in Canada? What is your destination? Do you have any firearms in your vehicle? Alcohol? Tobacco products?—and if, for whatever reason, one gives less than direct, satisfactory answers, one's vehicle will probably be searched by a uniformed officer wearing latex gloves who is trained to detect controlled substances and other contraband. Although the officer may be unfailingly polite, as most Canadians are, he will also exhibit a steely demeanor that sends a clear message to the casual visitor from the United States: You are entering our country now. We expect you to obey our laws and mind your manners.

Driving into Ontario, one unexpectedly loses an hour on the clock, the speed limit and other road signs are bilingual (English and French) and employ the metric system, and the highway is now called Queen's Route 61. (Yes, Canada is a member of the British Commonwealth, and Canadians are still the Queen's *subjects*.) Nevertheless, one feels comfortable cruising the two-laned highway toward Thunder Bay. The landscape is pastoral, and this is Canada, after all, a prosperous, modern Western democracy, not some squalid Third World dictatorship.

Traffic increases suddenly on the outskirts of Thunder Bay as Queen's Route 61 merges with Queen's Routes 11 and 17 to form the Thunder Bay Expressway, and one begins to see the inevitable signs of American cultural incursion: a Best Western motel, fast-food franchises, a Walmart. Ah, one thinks, Canada is not much different from the United States. And, I suppose, compared to many parts of the world, that is true. But if one spends enough time in the country, then one begins to sense, beneath the surface, a certain resistance to things American. In many respects Canada may share, or have adopted, American capitalist impulses, and Canada's fate as a nation may now be inextricably linked to that of the United States, but Canadians as a people seem to define themselves in opposition to the United States. Like siblings, the two peoples, born of the same parents, have grown differently while retaining a strong family resemblance. The United States is the big, oafish, but still mostly likable older brother—the high school jock—while Canada is intelligent, diffident, and sensitive—the kid brother who reads a lot and can't decide whether or not his older brother is a jerk. But somewhere deep down they know they have the same parents and must live in the same house.

* * *

Because Canada, Great Britain, and the United States have now been staunch allies for so long, it is difficult to imagine that things were ever any different. But in the aftermath of the American Revolution, the location of the boundary between Canada, still a British possession, and the new country known as the United States was a source of nearly sixty years of fierce disagreement and dispute. At that time the fur trade was flourishing, and success in the trade depended on access to the interior of the continent, where, particularly in the Rocky Mountains and much of Canada, the rivers and lakes teemed with fur-bearing mammals. This was the era of the voyageurs, those colorful and tough (and, some would add, generally uneducated and exploited) men, usually of French ancestry, who worked for large British companies—principally the North West Company—to reap the continent's rich harvest of fur.

At that time the North West Company primarily utilized the route westward that began on the northwestern shore of Lake Superior at Grand Portage, where the company constructed a large trading-post complex enclosed by wooden palisades. Grand Portage took its name from the initial eight-and-a-half-mile-long portage that climbed more than six hundred vertical feet from the lakeshore to intersect the Pigeon River above its impassable lower rapids and falls. From there the voyageurs paddled and portaged along what is now the international boundary between Minnesota and Ontario to the Lake of the Woods, and then down the Winnipeg River to Lake Winnipeg. At that point some struck out for the mountains to the west and north, while others followed the Red River of the North upstream (generally south) to the rich plains country of what is today Manitoba, Minnesota, and North and South Dakota.

At its peak in the 1790s the North West Company's stockade at Grand Portage contained sixteen buildings. Every year in late June the voyageurs rendezvoused here with the company's clerks and *bourgeois*, who had traveled in *maître* canoes (some of them thirty-five feet long and capable of carrying eight thousand pounds of cargo) from the company's headquarters in Montreal via a long and treacherous water route. The rendezvous, lasting most of July, was a raucous affair, as the voyageurs exchanged a year's worth of furs for muskets, traps, and other tools of the trade; manufactured goods like knives and copper kettles for trade with the Indians; brightly colored cloth (the voyageurs had their own distinctive fashion sense); and, of course, liquor.

But by the 1790s a political dispute was already threatening Grand Portage. In 1783 representatives of the newly formed United States and of his Britannic Majesty had signed the Definitive Treaty of Peace, also known as the Treaty of Paris, concluding the American Revolution. Article II of that treaty established the boundary between the United States and the remaining British possessions in North America. That boundary followed a line through the middle of Lakes Ontario, Erie, and Huron. Through Lake Superior, however, it followed a vaguely described line from Sault Sainte Marie "northward of the isles

Royal [Isle Royale] and Phelipeaux, to the Long Lake." On the 1755 map of North America used by the commissioners to negotiate the treaty, Long Lake appeared near the mouth of the Pigeon River. Unfortunately, Long Lake was a phantom—it did not (and does not) exist. Thus there was a substantial question as to whether Grand Portage was within the United States' or British territory. Acting in a manner that many Canadians still regard as quintessentially American, the United States began to assert jurisdiction over the site by requiring fur traders there to obtain American licenses and pay American customs duties. (In doing so, the United States ignored a provision in the 1794 Treaty of Amity, Commerce and Navigation between the two nations stating, "No duty of entry shall ever be levied by either party on peltries brought by land, or inland navigation into the said territories respectively." The United States' primary motivation in flouting that treaty provision was undoubtedly a desire to give Americans a leg up in their competition with the British companies.)

As a result of fierce competition with the Hudson's Bay Company, the North West Company's profit margins were already thin, and the payment of additional customs duties would have been disastrous. In 1803 the company gave up the fight, abandoning Grand Portage and relocating its main trading post forty miles northeast to the site of Fort William. In Lake Superior's harsh, damp climate the company's wooden stockade quickly decayed, and today nothing remains of the original structures. Instead, Grand Portage National Monument, located on the trading post's original site on land donated to the United States by the Grand Portage Band, contains a few reconstructed buildings where National Park Service interpreters in period costume provide a quiet glimpse into a noisy past.

The boundary dispute was not resolved until the Webster-Ashburton Treaty of 1842, which finally established the international boundary at the Pigeon River, while reserving the right of both countries' citizens to use "all water communications and all the usual portages along the line from Lake Superior to the Lake of the Woods, and also Grand portage, from the shore of Lake Superior to the Pigeon river, as actually used." The treaty came too late to save the North West Company, which had ceased to exist in 1821 when it merged with the Hudson's Bay Company, thus ending a rivalry that had helped open the continent.

* * *

Every city needs (though not every city has) a distinctive place for visitors to stay, a place that in some way embodies the history and personality of the locale. In Thunder Bay that place is the venerable and now somewhat threadbare Prince Arthur Hotel, located in downtown Port Arthur. Built in 1910-11 by the Canadian Pacific Railway, the six-story brick structure overlooks Water Street, the railroad tracks, the city marina, the breakwater, Thunder Bay itself, and, on the far side of the bay, the distant, palisaded Sibley Peninsula.

Notwithstanding the carefully selected quotations and photographs in its four-color brochure, the Prince Arthur was never a luxurious hostelry. It was built to provide comfortable and affordable accommodations for businessmen arriving in Port Arthur by train and for long-distance travelers laying-over for a night or two in town. Except for a few minor architectural details, the building itself is stolid and uninspiring; the lighting in the public areas and hallways is dim and institutional; and the furnishings in the recently remodeled rooms are similar to what one finds in midmarket hotel chains. My first stay at the Prince Arthur coincided with the 1998 Canadian Stand-Up Armwrestling Championship, held that year in Thunder Bay, and I often shared the elevator with one or more of the contestants—hulking (but polite) men with bulging, tattooed biceps, wearing tank tops and nylon jackets with beer logos on the back, smelling faintly of cigarette smoke, and often accompanied by their tough-cookie (but polite) girlfriends.

But—how can I explain it?—the Prince Arthur is eminently comfortable in a musty, down-at-the-heels sort of way. The construction, befitting an old railroad hotel, is bedrock-solid, and water gushes out of the bathroom faucet and showerhead as if it's powering a turbine in a hydroelectric plant (truly a novelty and luxury to someone from the American Southwest). Although the hotel is close to the railroad tracks, the solid walls muffle the sound so that the nearly continuous rumble and clatter of the trains becomes a soft, pleasant soundtrack to the sights of the city.

But perhaps what distinguishes the Prince Arthur more than anything else are the views from the waterside rooms. Looking out of the tall windows, one can survey the expanse of Thunder Bay from the Sibley Peninsula in the east to Mount McKay in the southwest. The middle view is to the southeast, and on clear, calm mornings the sunlight reflects brilliantly off the ultramarine water, sending quicksilver streams across its rippled surface. Freighters ride gently at anchor, and sailboats ply their way slowly across the limpid liquid medium. Even in fair weather wispy cirrus clouds often trail slowly across the pale-blue northern sky. Twenty miles across the bay, at the end of the Sibley Peninsula, the geologic formation known as the

Sleeping Giant reclines peacefully on the horizon. On such days the view from the Prince Arthur is unexpectedly lovely, even sublime.

The Prince Arthur also provides a convenient base for exploring the transitional area that is downtown Port Arthur. When I visited in 1998, the local Eaton's Department Store had recently closed, and the only viable businesses seemed to be fitness gyms, tanning salons, and travel agencies, all apparently catering to employees of the Ontario provincial government and Ontario Hydro who work in nearby office buildings. At night transients—many of them Canadian Indians from the nearby Fort William Indian Reserve—roamed the sidewalks in front of the empty storefronts, lending the otherwise deserted business district an exotic, rough-edged, even slightly menacing air.

When I returned two years later, a "charity casino" operated by the provincial government had opened a block west of the Prince Arthur, and the downtown seemed to be in the early stages of economic recovery. A couple of new restaurants were catering to casino patrons, and the sidewalks, though still not crowded, seemed friendlier. My room was on the fifth floor of the hotel, and after I opened my windows, I occasionally heard sounds of celebration and revelry issuing from the direction of the casino. In some ways I missed the dicey character of the old scene, but I found myself admiring the city's resilient character and I reminded myself that I did not come to Canada to experience the exotic, even if I am sometimes surprised by what I find.

* * *

Today Thunder Bay is reportedly home to the largest population of Finns in any city in the world outside of Finland. By some estimates as many as fifteen thousand Finns live in the city, most of them residing in an Old-World neighborhood near the intersection of Bay and Algoma Streets in Port Arthur. A distinctive commercial district radiates from the Bay-Algoma intersection. The stores here include the Kivela Bakery, Lauri's Hardware and Pawn Shop, Saasto's Men's Wear, Sirkka's Dressmaking, the Finnish Book Store, and, most interestingly, a store called Finnport, where one may buy sauna supplies, exquisite Finnish crystal, and commemorative ceramic plates illustrated with scenes from the *Kalevala*, an ancient, mythic tale generally regarded as the Finnish national epic. The heart of the Finnish business district, at 314 Bay Street, is a three-story brick-and-clapboard structure flanked by square towers and centered on an octagonal turret crowned by a cupola. Completed in 1910, this curious building is home to the Finlandia Club, the Finnish Building Company, the Finnish Labour Temple, and, a half-flight of stairs down from street level, the Hoito Restaurant, one of Thunder Bay's oldest eateries and a genuine cultural institution.

Hoito means "care" in Finnish. The Hoito Restaurant was established in 1918 as a cooperative to provide hearty, low-cost meals to Finnish workers—mostly lumberjacks—who came to Port Arthur from nearby bush camps to relax and socialize. Until the 1970s most regulars purchased meal tickets or paid a flat rate for all they could eat at communal tables. In the 1930s those meals cost sixty cents; in the 1960s, a dollar. In addition to standard diner fare (hamburgers, BLTs, etc.), the menu includes Finnish pancakes, Finnish wieners, fried Finnish sausages, salt fish, *viili* (clabbered milk), and *karjalan piirakka*

("Karelian pie," or rye crust filled with rice pudding or mashed potatoes). The portions are still ample, and today the full dinners, including beverage, bread, soup or salad, and dessert, cost eight to ten Canadian dollars.

Like many visitors to the city, during my first visit to Thunder Bay I eventually found my way to the Hoito. Eating alone in an unfamiliar restaurant can be an uncomfortable, even unnerving experience, but not at the Hoito. I arrived at the restaurant a bit after 7:00 p.m.—late by Hoito standards—and found a small table near the kitchen door. The communal tables were still crowded, but people had for the most part finished their meals and were simply chatting sociably with their neighbors, producing a pleasant hubbub in the room. Most of the other customers seemed to know each other and to be regulars, but they didn't regard me, a stranger, with suspicion. A few looked up as I walked in, acknowledged me with nods of their heads, and returned to their conversations. My waitress, a trim, attractive woman of indeterminate age—perhaps forty-five, perhaps ten years older than that—had obviously worked at the Hoito for a long time: her dress was feminine but sensible (knee-length skirt, dark stockings, comfortable shoes), her movements efficient but unhurried, her manner reserved but friendly. Her graying blonde hair was pulled into a short ponytail, revealing a lovely Nordic face—delicate features, creamy skin, Copenhagen-blue eyes—and, as if to let her beauty speak for itself, she wore no makeup or jewelry. Her serene demeanor seemed to reflect an inner calm and self-possession. As she patiently answered my questions about the Finnish dishes on the menu, her eyes glimmered with curiosity or mirth, but she asked no questions in return. I overheard her conversing in Finnish with customers at a nearby table, but I never even learned her name. She was probably a native of Canada, but in my mind she embodied the austere beauty and natural grace of her ancestral homeland.

On another visit I ate breakfast one Sunday morning at the Hoito's W-shaped counter. The counter is the domain mostly of older, single Finnish men with bronze complexions and brush-cut hair—more Hoito regulars. On this morning, however, I sat next to an amiable chap named Ken, who works as a machine oiler at a paper and pulp mill in the town of Red Rock, about a hundred kilometers northeast of Thunder Bay. Ken has thinning hair, an aquiline nose, and careworn, friendly eyes. He drives to Thunder Bay every weekend to spend a day with his twelve-year-old daughter, who lives here with his former wife. Ken has worked at the mill on and off for many years but has drifted from job to job—at the mill and elsewhere—and seems vaguely dissatisfied with his lot in life. Between jobs he has returned to school several times to try to earn a degree—he struck me as someone who would be an enthusiastic but unfocused student—but has reluctantly given up that idea. Now he seems preoccupied with the usual concerns of middle-aged men: his daughter's education, his health, his retirement savings. When he learned I was from the United States, he became quite animated, his manner expressing equal parts curiosity, respect, and envy. The United States, for Ken, is an almost mythical land of better jobs, higher wages, and warmer weather—the tantalizing land of milk and honey that, with the current exchange rate, he can't afford even to visit for more than a day. I suddenly felt sheepish about my own good fortune—the accident of my birth. But I was relieved to see that Ken apparently was unaware of my discomfiture. As we ate our breakfasts, he continued chattering about his life in a self-effacing, almost neurotic manner—quite charmingly really—and I soon found myself sharing his everyday concerns, nodding at his modest ambitions, and feeling an unexpected kinship with him.

* * *

One of Thunder Bay's most attractive features, for me at least, is its proximity to wild places. I am not a paddler and so am not referring to Quetico Provincial Park and the rest of the Boundary Waters west of the city. And I am not a fisherman or hunter and so am not referring to the myriad lakes and vast boreal forests of northwestern Ontario (located in large part on publicly owned "Crown Lands") where men and women engage in an atavistic battle of wits with wild animals. But I am an avid camper, hiker, and trail runner, and I enjoy watching wildlife. So when I visit Thunder Bay, I always set aside a couple of days to spend on the tip of the Sibley Peninsula, at Sleeping Giant Provincial Park.

Ontario maintains an impressive system of provincial parks that often combine the best of two worlds: frontcountry with well-tended campgrounds and recreational facilities; and backcountry that is extensive, wild, and relatively untended. The campground at Sleeping Giant is located on the forested, ferny shore of Marie Louise Lake, a large inland lake with a sandy swimming beach and a near view of the palisades of the Sleeping Giant itself. In the evening, if one is lucky, one hears, across the water, the loon's otherworldly call. But the campground itself is a relatively civilized place, with a large, modern visitor center and comfort stations with flush toilets, hot showers, and laundry facilities. Despite the amenities, its summer season is short.

When I've camped there in late September, the visitor center and comfort stations have already closed for the year; several of the camping loops have been barricaded; and the notices of interpretive programs posted on the bulletin boards are a couple of weeks out of date. The park rangers—or wardens, as they are called in Canada—are invisible, perhaps taking a break after the busy summer season, and the entire campground has a deserted, melancholy feel.

Even in late September, however, the popular campsites on the shore of Marie Louise Lake tend to fill by late afternoon. Because I adhere to the rule that when staying in a developed campground, one should stay as far away from other people as possible—campgrounds are generally close quarters, and I have no interest in observing my neighbors' peculiar personal habits (or in having them observe mine)—I tend to camp on higher ground, in the woods above the lake. There, sitting quietly at my picnic table in a thicket of balsam fir, paper birch, mountain maple, and round-leaved dogwood, I've glimpsed a red fox (with a strange, mottled coat), a black-bear cub, and an unidentified fur-bearing mammal that might have been a marten or fisher.

Sleeping Giant also has an extensive trail system that, even more than the rest of the park, is deserted in late September and that draws me into the backcountry. I particularly like to run slowly out the Kabeyun Trail along Tee Harbor and Lehtinen's Bay before scrambling over car-sized boulders and climbing up a chimney in the hard, diabase cliffs to the bent knees of the supine Sleeping Giant. The flat summit, with a forest of wind-stunted trees (mostly balsam firs, white spruces, and aspens), tufts of windblown grass, and outcrops of lichen-encrusted rock, has an open, airy feel, similar to what one experiences at timberline in high mountains. From that vantage point, about eight hundred feet above Lake Superior, one can look south to Isle Royale or, pivoting to the west, across the bay to the city of Thunder Bay on the far shore. The passage from the lake into the bay between the feet of the Sleeping Giant and Pie Island resembles a broad fjord. On a breezy day, with the watery scent of the big lake in the air, it is an invigorating prospect.

Today the provincial park occupies most but not all the Sibley Peninsula. Near a point of land on the peninsula's southeastern side is the small settlement of Silver Islet Landing, once a raucous mining town and now a picturesque seasonal community of refurbished miners' cabins and modern vacation cottages. During the summer the original Silver Islet Store, located adjacent to the community dock, still sells groceries and other supplies, but otherwise the town is blessedly free of commercial development. Silver Islet Landing takes its name from a small island composed of Animikie slates located about a mile offshore. Historian Grace Lee Nute evocatively described the island as resembling "a human skull, about ninety feet each way." At its highest point it rises only eight feet above the lake's normal level.

For about fifteen years, beginning in 1868, Silver Islet was the location of the world's richest silver mine, as miners followed a twenty-foot-wide vein of pure silver from the island's surface to more than twelve hundred feet beneath the lakebed. Even by the standards of the day, the work was extraordinarily hazardous. Coal-fired pumps worked constantly to dewater the leaky shafts, and because swells occasionally washed over the tiny island, the mining company constructed a large cribbed-timber breakwater, ten times the size of the island, around its most exposed sides. Inside this sheltered area the company erected an elaborate complex that included machine, blacksmith, and carpenter shops; storehouses and boardinghouses; private quarters and clubrooms; offices; a lighthouse; and ore-shipping docks. By the time the mine closed in 1884, reduced to unprofitability by high overhead and diminishing yield, it had produced $3.25 million worth of silver—about $100 million in 2023 dollars.

I haven't visited Silver Islet, but I've sat on the community dock at the landing on a brisk fall day, looking at the choppy water in the nearby channel, water stirred to an aquamarine hue by a cool breeze off the lake; and I've pondered the mysterious geologic processes that injected a molten stream of silver into fissures in an inert mass of gray slates; contemplated the time that passed as the valuable lode solidified in its secret, interstitial space; imagined the prospectors' euphoria when they discovered the treasure's eroded hiding place, and the miners' fatigue and fear as they performed their back-breaking work in dark, frigid passages beneath the lakebed; considered the possibilities of accident, explosion, hypothermia, or drowning—the quickness of death in these northern climes; and reflected on the brutal reality of men risking their lives to extract from the earth's crust the precious metal from which other men—those dining on white linen tablecloths in faraway cities—derived their fortunes.

* * *

Just east of Thunder Bay along Queen's Routes 11 and 17 is a rest area, situated on a small hill above the highway, offering distant views of the city and bay. The rest area itself is dominated by a larger-than-life bronze statue of the young

Canadian man after whom it is named, Terry Fox. In ways difficult for an outsider to understand, Terry Fox looms large in the Canadian psyche, and even today, more than forty years after his death, his story resonates deeply with the Canadian people.

Born in Winnipeg, Manitoba, and raised in a suburb of Vancouver, British Columbia, Terry was a healthy, active boy who grew into a shy, hard-working adolescent. He applied himself diligently to his schoolwork and dedicated himself to his favorite sport, basketball. If anything distinguished him, it was his extraordinary determination. Although he was less than six feet tall and had little natural ability, by virtue of long, hard practice he starred on his high school's basketball team and later, as a college freshman, walked on and made the team at Simon Fraser University.

In 1977, after his first year at university, he was diagnosed with bone cancer, and his right leg was amputated six inches above the knee.

On the night before his leg was amputated, his high school basketball coach brought him a magazine with an article about an amputee who had run the New York City Marathon. That night Terry decided, in his own words, "to meet this new challenge head on and not only overcome my disability, but conquer it in such a way that I could never look back and say it disabled me." Terry's particular vision was to run across Canada, raising $1 million for cancer research along the way. He was haunted by the people he had met in the cancer clinic, the ones who survived and the ones who didn't. "My quest would not be a selfish one," he wrote to prospective sponsors. "I could not leave knowing these faces and feelings would still exist, even though I would be set free from mine. Somewhere the hurting must stop . . . and I was determined to take myself to the limit for this cause."

After undergoing sixteen months of chemotherapy, Terry began training for what he called the "Marathon of Hope." Although the Canadian Cancer Society was initially skeptical of his proposal, his persistence eventually earned its sponsorship. On April 12, 1980, he dipped his artificial leg into the Atlantic Ocean at Saint John's, Newfoundland, and began running west. His prosthesis thudded on the pavement, his gait was awkward and unbalanced, and his face often betrayed the strain of his effort, but on he ran, averaging forty-two kilometers a day—a marathon a day—for 143 consecutive days. His route took him through Nova Scotia, Prince Edward Island, New Brunswick, Québec, and Ontario. News of his epic run spread, people began to line his route, and donations poured in to the Canadian Cancer Society. On September 1, 1980, however, just outside of Thunder Bay, he grew weak and was forced to stop. He had neglected his scheduled check-ups—perhaps he had sensed the inevitability of his disease—and doctors discovered that the cancer had metastasized to his lungs. Ten months later, on June 28, 1981, one month short of his twenty-third birthday, Terry Fox died. Before his death, however, people had contributed more than $24 million to his Marathon of Hope—about one dollar for each Canadian alive at the time. As of 2016 more than $715 million had been donated for cancer research in Terry's name.

Terry Fox's story is inspirational in the best sense of that word. Here was a likeable young man struck down by a fatal disease. Here was a young man who literally expended his life's energy fighting the disease that afflicted him. His undisguised suffering seemed to be symbolic of the suffering of the human race, and his attitude and determination in the face of that suffering was quietly heroic. But that, by itself, does not adequately account for his place in Canadians' hearts and minds. With his vision of running across Canada in the cause of combating human suffering, Terry Fox ignored the political and linguistic barriers that divide modern Canada—rendered those barriers inconsequential—and unwittingly tapped into a nascent Canadian nationalism. Terry's personality seemed to be a distinctively Canadian type—quiet, hard-working, and self-effacing—and the fact that he was born in a prairie province, was raised in British Columbia, and began his run in Newfoundland enhanced his Pan-Canadian persona. Canadians everywhere embraced him as one of their own, held him up as an exemplar of what was best in their culture and nation. Terry Fox became the mythic Canadian Everyman. That image has persisted. In a 1999 poll sponsored by the *National Post*, responders selected Terry Fox as Canada's "greatest hero."

When I ask my young, hip, well-dressed waitress at Bistro One in Thunder Bay what two or three things a visitor to town should be sure to do, she pauses and bites her lower lip pensively for a minute. Then she answers quietly, in a voice edged with emotion, "You should visit the Terry Fox overlook. Do you know who he was? What he did may not seem like much to an American, but to us Canadians, it's pretty important."

* * *

Each time I visit Thunder Bay and stay in the Prince Arthur Hotel, I try, at least one morning, to get up early and drive northeast along Cumberland Street, past the derelict mom-and-pop motels built during the post-World War II travel boom, to

Boulevard Lake Park, where I like to run slowly on the paved trail that encircles the lake. On weekdays the park is deserted but for a few neighborhood walkers, and the morning stillness is broken only by the sounds of ducks quacking sociably on the water and Canada geese milling warily along the shore.

Near the southern end of Boulevard Lake Park are three modern apartment buildings, six or seven stories high, whose architecture recalls many other institutional buildings in Thunder Bay and, indeed, throughout Canada. Their common design is uninspired and monotonous—the exterior pattern of small windows and cramped porches indicates that each apartment has the same floor plan—and their exterior facades consist of painted cinder blocks. The cars in the parking lots tend to be older-model sedans, their fenders and wheel wells perforated by rust. Although I've never confirmed this fact, the buildings appear to be smaller versions of the monolithic public-housing projects one finds in larger cities in the United States. The buildings' relatively small scale, however, renders them less forbidding than their American counterparts and reminds me that today Canada has a population of about thirty-five million people, or about one tenth as many as the United States. (The United States had a population of about thirty-five million at the end of the Civil War.) Although thirty-five million is a substantial number and although I am suspicious of simple explanations of complex phenomena, Canada does not yet seem to have crossed that demographic line beyond which a modern governmental bureaucracy must treat its citizens as fungible goods to function effectively. In Canada an individual human life still seems to matter.

The apartment buildings near Boulevard Lake Park also reflect certain socialist tendencies that seem to be more prominent in Canadian than American culture. From national health care to enhanced educational opportunities to subsidized housing, the Canadian government does more to assist its citizens to attain and maintain a high quality of life than the American government does for its citizens. Canadians are justifiably proud of the fact that the United Nations has consistently rated Canada as having the highest quality of life in the world. All of which causes me to think about the significant cultural differences between two nations that, geographically, historically, and linguistically, have as much in common as any two nations in the world.

The United States and Canada have closely intertwined histories. Both were born of the centuries-long rivalry between England and France for dominance in world affairs, a rivalry that manifested itself in the New World as a struggle for control of the area between Hudson Bay and the Ohio River. Although the first European settlement along the Saint Lawrence River was French—Samuel de Champlain established a trading post at Québec in 1608, one year after Captain John Smith and a group of English colonists had founded the settlement at Jamestown, Virginia—and although French influence remains strong in eastern Canada, France formally ceded to England most of its possessions in the New World east of the Mississippi River in 1763, after the French and Indian War. Thus, at the time of the American Revolution, all of eastern North America, except Florida (which was claimed by Spain), was in British possession. During the revolution, however, British colonists above the Great Lakes remained loyal to the British Crown, and nearly forty thousand Tories fled northward from the rebellious colonies. After the revolution there was residual antipathy between the United States and the remaining British possessions to the north. During the War of 1812 American forces tried several times unsuccessfully to invade Canada, finally sacking York (Toronto) out of frustration.

The Dominion of Canada was created on July 1, 1867, when the British Parliament recognized the federation of Nova Scotia, New Brunswick, Lower Canada (Québec), and Upper Canada (Ontario) as a self-governing entity. Like the United States, the new nation grew quickly, purchasing the Hudson's Bay Company's immense western territories in 1869 and securing British Columbia in 1871 with a promise to construct a transcontinental railroad. Today Canada is a federation of ten provinces and three territories (including the Inuit-governed Arctic territory of Nunavut, carved out of the Northwest Territories in 1999). Geographically it is the second-largest nation in the world and shares an almost four-thousand-mile-long border with the United States.

I don't know enough even to speculate about the continuing antagonism between Canadians of British and French ancestry. Rather, the question that interests me, especially after several recent visits to Canada, is why British colonists in Canada remained loyal to Great Britain during the American Revolution, and why Canada has remained a part of the Commonwealth, while the British colonists in America rebelled against the mother country and founded a new, independent nation. And why Canadian culture has retained a more European flavor than American culture. In so many ways—from its treatment of its native peoples to its low violent-crime rate to its government's focus on the health and well-being of its citizens—Canada is—dare I say it?—more civilized than the United States. (I recall a conversation with a Canadian family at Pukaskwa National Park. The oldest boy, aged twelve, interrogated me relentlessly about Americans' fascination with handguns. Do you own a gun? he asked. Do you know anyone who does? Why do they have guns? What are they afraid of? I felt like a visitor from a distant, violence-ridden planet.)

One obvious reason is demographics. Settled predominantly by conservative, white, middle-class British subjects (including many Scots), English-speaking Canada today is predominantly a conservative, white, middle-class country. The eastern seaboard of the United States, on the other hand, was settled by a diverse—some might say motley— assortment of British colonists—well-to-do planters and merchants, political discontents, religious refugees, indentured servants, and debtors. And that diversity only increased as the United States acquired Spain's and later Mexico's territories in North America north of present-day Mexico. Moreover, perhaps partly in reaction to its southern neighbor's relatively open immigration policy and the chaos that policy occasionally engenders, Canada has historically regulated immigration more closely than the United States. Until recent years the huddled masses were not particularly welcome north of the border. Finally, Canada's climate doesn't support the cultivation of cotton, rice, or tobacco, the three labor-intensive crops that flourished in the American South and that fueled the slave trade in this country. As a result of all those factors, Canada today is more racially and ethnically homogeneous than the United States. Racial and ethnic homogeneity tend to encourage cultural conformity, which, although it doesn't eliminate criminal behavior, often acts to suppress it. On the other hand, America sometimes seems to me less a melting pot than a vat of volatile chemicals. At times the chemicals combine magically to produce beautiful, surreal colors; at other times they react in violent explosion.

Another reason, also obvious but often overlooked, is climate. Because most of Canada is located north of 48° latitude and because its interior provinces are located far from the ocean's moderating influence, its climate is marked by dramatic fluctuations in temperature, both diurnally and seasonally. As everyone knows, Canadian winters are long and frigid, occasionally even life-threatening. (White River, Ontario, fifty miles northeast of Lake Superior, proudly—or perversely—advertises itself as the "coldest spot in Canada." In 1935 the temperature here reportedly plummeted to -72°F.) During the country's formative years, when people lived closer to the bone, Canada's extreme climate undoubtedly imposed on them subtle pressure to cooperate to survive. And just as surely its influence continues today, even with modern technology to help insulate people from the climate's rigors. If people occasionally must impose on their neighbors to jump-start their cars in the winter, then they are probably inclined to treat their neighbors politely and to reciprocate as necessary. Common hardship fosters cooperation, which in turn encourages civility and a sense that we are all in this thing together. Is it really so difficult to believe that climate affects our social behavior?

Certain cultural developments have also served, unintentionally, to differentiate the two nations. In the United States mass media—particularly television and popular movies—have perpetuated and exaggerated America's image of itself as a nation of tough-talking, rugged individualists. The media (and, I must add, various politicians) have mythologized Americans' desire for political independence and personal freedom—an integral part of our origin story and national character—and co-opted it for their own purposes. Meanwhile, Canada has evolved in a more orderly and less flamboyant fashion, respecting an Old-World tradition that values social cohesion and the political commonweal. In America, the individual was and is supreme; in Canada, the community.

In the end, though, no one—not the most knowledgeable historian or sociologist, and certainly not I—can adequately account for the cultural differences between Canada and the United States. Just as siblings may grow apart while retaining a family resemblance, so sometimes do nations. Genetics and environment both play significant but ultimately indefinable roles in the differentiation of individuals. It must be enough for me, then, to mark the differences here, to try to be sensitive to them, and to bear them in mind when I venture across our northern border.

* * *

During my last visit to Thunder Bay I went in search of a gift to take home to my wife and ended up at a store called Take a Hike in downtown Fort William. Take a Hike is owned by a woman named Diane Petryna and sells sportswear primarily for women. The store's interior is decorated to remind one of an outdoor landscape: the ceiling is painted sky blue, and the walls are covered in murals of lush mountainscapes. Toward the back of the store, in an area framed and furnished to resemble the interior of a log cabin, Diane also sells outdoor-related gifts: moose and bear figurines, CDs of music inspired by the natural sounds of the North Woods, scented candles and soap. On the day I stopped in, the store was being tended by Diane and one of her employees, a shy young man named Sean. Sean is a student at Lakehead University and had recently finished a stint as a seasonal warden at Sleeping Giant Provincial Park. As I was looking at some fleece jackets, he and I chatted agreeably about the park and his work there. (At one point, when I looked toward the gift-shop area of the store, Sean smiled sheepishly, shook his head, and, glancing at Diane, whispered, "I try to avoid going back there.")

Sean needed to unpack some new inventory, so I soon found myself in Diane's capable hands. Diane is fortyish, with a round, pretty face; a creamy complexion; short hair the color of maple syrup; and warm brown eyes. She seems genuinely—and I use this word reluctantly, because I do not intend the blandness and condescension it often connotes—nice. And in that way she seemed to me representative of many people I had met in Canada. Her politeness was not a mere business affectation but seemed to flow from a wellspring of feeling and belief: gratitude to her customers; respect for other human beings; faith that people are, at bottom, decent; and a conviction that one should treat other people as one wants and expects to be treated. It is a mode of human interaction that demands time and energy and that is necessarily diminished or lost in a setting or society that prioritizes business efficiency, transactional volume, and profit margin.

Diane showed me several stylish jackets that, she mentioned with obvious pride, were made in Canada. But I had trouble making up my mind, so she finally offered to model them for me, because, as she said, sometimes it helps to see how they look on a real person. Then she put on the jackets one after another and walked slowly into the middle of the store, smiling self-consciously as she turned and with deliberate movements placed one hand on her hip, so that I, a stranger and an American, could appreciate the patterns of the fabrics—North Woods designs of moose and fir trees and snowflakes—the quality of the materials, and the cut of each garment.

# # #

Schreiber, Ontario:
Flesh and Spirit in the
Canadian Shield

I don't know what prevents me from roasting you with
this torch.

Aristophanes, *Lysistrata*

The Canadian Shield is a complex mass of igneous and metamorphic rock, dark and hard, that extends from the arctic tundra and Inuit communities of north central Canada to the boreal forests and timber and mining towns of the Lake Superior region, nearly encircling Hudson Bay and constituting almost half Canada's surface area. Shield rock is Archaean, dating to nearly four billion years old, and the shield itself is the most extensive area of Precambrian rock exposed on the earth's surface. J. Tuzo Wilson, an eminent Canadian geologist, once described it as the "frigid heart and solid foundation" of the North American continent.

Its landforms eroded across eons of time, the Shield today is a vast area of low relief and imperfect drainage, dotted with innumerable lakes and swamps occupying small glaciated depressions and basins. Winters are long and baleful; summers, short and buggy. The southern portion of the shield, heavily forested, has always resisted settlement and acted as a barrier to travel between eastern and western Canada. It is a dark and confusing landscape, where myriad trees obscure landmarks and views, and muskeg (*terre tremblant* in French) makes for difficult passage. Except along the comparatively hospitable shores of the larger lakes, the Ojibwe and Cree Indians avoided it, and even today only narrow, two-laned highways cut through the seemingly endless taiga. Shield rock, here highly mineralized, produces much of Canada's metallic wealth—iron, copper, zinc, molybdenum, uranium, silver, gold, and platinum—and the towns scattered across the landscape—towns like Manitouwadge and Hornepayne, Ontario—are tough company towns that exist only to extract the region's valuable natural resources.

Queen's Route 17, a segment the Trans-Canada Highway—Canada's primary east-west traffic artery—and the Canadian Pacific Railway cross the southern portion of the Shield, along the northern shoreline of Lake Superior. But even the highway and railroad have not attracted many immigrants. Between Sault Sainte Marie, on the east, and Thunder Bay, on the west, a distance of about 440 miles, the largest town is Marathon, population 4,791. The highway carries a heavy volume of big-truck traffic, but it is for the most part only two lanes wide, with occasional passing lanes on the longer uphill grades. It is a treacherous road.

As one drives the Trans-Canada Highway east from Thunder Bay, Lake Superior, here at its widest, stretches away beyond the southern horizon. Its surface glitters and dazzles in the morning sun. Yet, surprisingly, one finds oneself looking left more than right, more to the dark, brooding forest than to the lake's light, shimmering surface. Where the muskeg predominates, the forest consists of unmixed stands of tufted black spruce. Rooted in bog, draped in epiphytic moss, and preternaturally uniform in height, the trees, dark in silhouette, scratch the pale northern sky. Primordial and inhuman, this forest inspires a deep foreboding, a feeling that seems to rise, like a vapor, from the peat of ancient, perhaps archetypal, memory. Indeed, this landscape seems a remnant of an antediluvian time, when the earth was inchoate and society tribal, and the world witnessed epic battles between good and evil, and God appeared in the heavens to deliver His message to the chosen and smite the unholy, and men were riven by the competing forces of their own nature—called by the spirit and tempted by the flesh.

* * *

Schreiber, Ontario, is a hard-bitten town of 1,788 souls, perched atop Lake Superior, enveloped by the dark, somber hills of the Canadian Shield. Established in the 1880s as a camp for workers constructing the Canadian Pacific Railway, Schreiber— locally pronounced "Skry-ber"—is still a gritty railroad town (though no longer a CPR divisional headquarters, as it once was). It is also a convenient way station on the Trans-Canada

Highway, and both trains and trucks rumble and rattle through town at all hours of the day and night.

Today the population of the town is overwhelmingly white and blue-collar. According to Statistics Canada, other than a small number of "aborigines" (Canadian Indians), fewer than ten people in Schreiber are members of a "visible minority." Only half the town's adult population has completed high school, and less than one in twenty university. The average income is Can$31,000.

My complimentary visitor map of northwestern Ontario contains the following polite, even optimistic, description of Schreiber:

> Nestled in a valley surrounded by rugged hills, lies this quaint little town of 1,600 people. Located on Highway 17 this would be a very sound choice as a stopover location as you travel the region. One of the oldest communities on the North Shore of Lake Superior. Always known as a railroad centre, you can still hear the eary [*sic*; probably not an intentional pun], lonesome sound of the train whistle as they continuously echo against the surrounding hills. To appreciate Schreiber's history, visitors should tour downtown to view two plaques which commemorate "Sir Collingwood Schreiber" and the "Japanese Canadians" who were relocated to road camps in 1942. View the rail yard and the historic C. P. Rail Station. See the restored 1955 yard engine [locomotive] or sit in an authentic motor car.

Schreiber, Ontario

What truly distinguishes Schreiber from other towns in this part of Ontario, however, is its unusually large population of Italian-Canadians. Italians immigrated to Canada to work on the railroad and in the mines (as they often did to the United States), and a disproportionate number, it seems, settled in Schreiber. Today fully half the town's population claims Italian ancestry. Most of Schreiber's residents, in fact, trace their roots to a single town, Siderno, in the Calabria region of southern Italy, on the toe of the Italian boot. The Schreiber telephone book runs the alphabet in Italian surnames: Cebrario, Commisso, Costa, Diano, Figliomeni (nineteen listings), Maggio, Pasqualino, Pellegrino, Spadoni, Speziale, Valentino, and Veneziano. The local bar is Rocco's, and the restaurant generally acknowledged as the best in town is Rosie and Josie, a pleasant *trattoria* serving homemade spaghetti and other traditional southern Italian fare.

The presence of the Italians in northwestern Ontario is curious. After viewing Schreiber in winter, one would be hard-pressed to imagine a less likely setting for an enclave of people from the Mediterranean. The frozen wastes of the Canadian Shield seem hostile even to the notion of *la dolce vita*.

* * *

I am circumnavigating Lake Superior by car. After spending a pleasant night at the Rossport Inn, an old railroad hotel located in the quaint village of Rossport (and now owned by a Hemingwayesque American expatriate named Ned Basher), I have started driving toward Pukaskwa National Park, about seventy-five miles east, intending to camp for a couple of nights. Shopping in the hinterlands of northwestern Ontario can be a dicey proposition, and when, four miles west of Schreiber, I see a Can-Op service station prominently advertising "Groceries" on its outside wall, I decide to stop to buy gas and supplies. The store occupies the same building as the Fallen Rock Restaurant, a derelict, windowless roadhouse now apparently down for the count, and shares an immense gravel parking lot with the adjacent Filane's Fallen Rock Motel, an ell-shaped, two-story building of cinder-block construction and vaguely Tudor design.

When I walk inside the store to pay for the gas, I quickly realize I won't be buying any food or supplies here: except for a depleted selection of soft drinks, bottled water, candy, snack food, and postcards, the shelves and racks of the small store are empty, and the interior is given over mostly to empty space and a diner counter, behind which an attendant—a tall, rangy, sallow-faced older gentleman wearing a plaid shirt, a quilted vest, and a baseball cap—stands solemn guard. The linoleum floor is chipped and stained; the counters, shelves, and fixtures are dusty and decrepit; and the whole place—the whole enterprise—seems moribund. The attendant watches me silently and, I feel, suspiciously as I inspect the meager wares.

For a minute I think the store might be in the process of going out of business. Then I notice an expensive Yamaha sound mixer, coated with a heavy layer of dust, stashed in a corner behind the counter. I also notice, displayed haphazardly on the shelves and counters, record albums and cassette tapes by a singer named Cosimo Filane. I pick up and study a vinyl LP titled "This Is It!" The sun-faded jacket photograph shows Mr. Filane standing in front of the Fallen Rock Motel. He is wearing a white shirt, a dark sport coat with wide lapels, and plaid pants; his left arm, cigarette in hand, is stretched toward the listener; and his right arm is cocked like a quarterback's, with the thumb pointing backward toward the motel. The album features covers of 1970s-era pop tunes like "Behind Closed Doors," "Tie a Yellow Ribbon," and "Bad Bad Leroy Brown," as well as some songs with unfamiliar titles that appear to be Mr. Filane's original compositions. The store also stocks and sells dusty hardcover copies of a novel by Mr. Filane titled *You Can't Win Them All*, published in 1986 by Fallen Rock Productions.

Despite my better instincts, I am beginning to be intrigued by this man named Cosimo Filane. Finally putting two and two together, I ask the attendant, who has been watching me silently, if Mr. Filane owns the service station.

The attendant smiles sardonically without showing his teeth, then moves his bulbous lips silently for a couple of seconds. Finally he says quietly, "Yeah, Mr. Big." And he nods his head toward a door behind the counter that communicates with a tiny, cluttered office, in which, I now realize, a man is speaking on the telephone in an animated voice. He is saying something about bottled water.

Is that Mr. Filane? I ask.

The attendant nods again.

At that moment Cosimo Filane ends his telephone conversation and appears suddenly behind the counter. He is a short, robust man, with an olive complexion, brown eyes, full lips, and a shock of thick, wavy dark-brown hair surprising for a man in his fifties. He is wearing a leather jacket, polyester pants, and leather shoes with metal buckles. A gold pinkie ring flashes on his right hand, and a gold bracelet glitters on his left wrist.

"I'm headin' down to the Cosiana, Al," he announces jovially. "I'll be back after lunch." Al the attendant nods but doesn't say anything. Then, as Mr. Filane heads out the door, he smiles in my direction and offers me a hearty "Good morning!"

After he exits, I ask Al if he thinks Mr. Filane would be willing to talk to me about life in Schreiber.

Al moves his mouth for a minute without saying anything, as if he is literally chewing his cud. "Oh, I'm sure he would," he says finally. "The trick would be getting him to shut up."

* * *

As I approach the town limits of Schreiber a few minutes later, a billboard welcomes me to the "Home of Domenic Filane, Canadian Boxing Champion / 1990 Commonwealth Games / 1992 Barcelona Olympics." Then, as I cruise slowly through town—which appears to be a typical Canadian North Woods burg—I pass Filane's Tempo Variety Store/Can-Op service station, Filane's Coin Car Wash, and Filane's Cosiana Inn. That evening, while sitting at my campsite in Pukaskwa National Park, I notice that the brand of the bottled water I purchased at the Can-Op is Filane's Canadian Spring Water, "Eau de source naturelle," and that the logo on the label features, instead of an apostrophe, a jaunty musical note. It seems that the Filanes are either Schreiber's first family or its most shameless self-promoters. Or, perhaps, both.

* * *

It is two years later, and I have returned to the Schreiber area as part of another trip to Lake Superior's northern shore. Fittingly, I begin my visit by stopping to buy gas at the Can-Op four miles west of town. When I enter the store, I am surprised—though I don't know why I should be—to find Al still tending the place. Standing silently behind the counter, he looks the same as he did two years ago: tall, thin, and sallow, with a jowly, almost hangdog face and a stoical attitude. His appearance is spectral, ethereal. He is again wearing—or still wearing—a plaid shirt and quilted vest, the uniform of the North Woods. His hair, the color and texture of steel wool, sprays out from under a dirty baseball cap, worn, intentionally or otherwise, slightly askew. He has an eccentric, almost comical, aspect. If a spirit, at least he seems a benign one.

After I pay for the gas, I again inspect the Cosimo Filane merchandise on display in the store. As far as I can tell, it's the same merchandise I saw two years ago.

Al watches me for a minute before asking, "Are you visiting the area?"

I tell him yes, I plan to be in the area for a couple of days.

"Where are you from?"

When I say New Mexico, in the American Southwest, he pauses and almost smiles. "Twenty years ago I visited Arizona," he says. "I drove down there in the spring to see the desert in bloom and to take photographs. It was beautiful. I spent a month just traveling around. Phoenix, Tucson, a place called Organ Pipe Cactus National Monument."

He forms his words slowly and carefully, with a slight thickness in his voice, as if he has a perpetually dry mouth. His tongue works constantly to moisten his lips. His steel-blue eyes are clouded with cataracts, and he is afflicted by a slight palsy. Despite his infirmities, however, he has a calm, even noble air. His gaze is steady, and his posture erect, almost military. We chat for a few minutes about his long-ago trip to the Southwest.

As he talks, I find myself studying one of Cosimo Filane's record albums. When he finishes, I tell him that his employer, Mr. Filane, seems to be a man of many talents.

"He thinks so," Al responds dryly. "Yeah, he thinks he's a real Renaissance man."

Al is evidently unimpressed by Cosimo's various endeavors. He is quiet for a minute, and I can sense him deciding whether or not to continue. Then, apparently having made up his mind, he says, "But it's all show, all image. Even his name. His real name isn't Filane. It's Figliomeni. But one of his singing idols was Frankie Laine, so he adopted the name Filane—a contraction of Figliomeni and Laine. He's not a very good speller. Guess who his other idol is, or was." Al cocks his head, looks at me out of the corners of his eyes, spreads his arms, and leans forward, as if to embrace an audience. The gesture is vaguely familiar, but I can't quite place it.

"Dino," he says, when he realizes I won't get it. "Dean Martin. He wants to be a big-time Vegas entertainer. But he's just a lounge singer, and not a very good one at that." Al pauses. "He thinks he's a tenor—a great Italian tenor—and he tends to pick songs written for tenors. The problem is, he's a baritone with a one-octave range. You should see him straining to hit the high notes. He looks like he's got lockjaw.

"But he's Italian, there's no doubt about that. You should see him when a young woman pulls into the station. He hustles out, pumps her gas, smiles and flirts with her. But if it's a man, he just sits inside and lets him pump his own gas."

As Al talks, I perch on one of the counter stools, and he finally asks if I'd like a cup of coffee. The Bunn-O-Matic seems to be the only functioning appliance in the kitchen. As he pours me a cup, I comment on the Yamaha sound mixer, still occupying a dusty corner behind the counter.

Al shakes his head. "It's Cosimo's. He always buys the best of everything. The problem is, he never takes the time to learn how to use anything properly. He spent thousands of dollars on that thing, but all he can do is twirl the knobs. He plays with it until he likes the sound, but he has no idea what he's doing. He doesn't know the difference between crescendo and diminuendo.

"But that's his modus operandi. Spend, don't think. You wouldn't believe the money he wastes. Look at that computer and laser printer," he says, pointing to two other pieces of dusty, derelict equipment behind the counter. "He bought the most expensive ones on the market at the time, but he didn't do any research before he wrote the check. That fancy laser printer won't print spreadsheets. So I have to do the business's spreadsheets on my dot matrix printer at home.

"He never learned that you don't buy a Rolls-Royce to go grocery shopping."

It is difficult to describe, but, despite the uniformly critical things Al is saying about Cosimo, his employer, to me, a stranger, I sense no hostility in the words. On the contrary, I find myself thinking that, despite appearances, the two men might actually be friends in some fashion. After all, some interesting architecture is based on the concept of opposing forces. For his part, Al evidently sees himself as Cosimo's conscience and, perhaps, savior.

As I sit at the counter drinking my coffee, which is surprisingly good, I pick up and peruse a copy of Cosimo's novel, *You Can't Win Them All*. A color brochure tucked inside the front cover describes a plot that sounds suspiciously like embellished autobiography:

> When Tony Caruso, an ex-hockey player turned singer toured Northern Ontario to promote his new album, he had no idea what was in store for him when he met Dean Filane in the little known town of Fallen Rock. Dean was the coach of a Minor Hockey Team and enjoyed the challenge that his Team, the Filane Flyers, offered, but when the roof of the arena in town was condemned, the coach found an even greater challenge when he tried to raise money to have the problem remedied. His opponent was Henry Peabody, a wily lawyer who had a vested interest in building a new arena and who proved to be a formidable adversary.

The book jacket quotes a critic named Richard Rohmer as saying, "Filane's Blood and Gut story from Northern Ontario of a Northern Ontario lad trying to get into the cruel, real world of hockey is a true-to-life good read." Al watches me for a minute as I study the book, and then smiles slyly. When I put the book on the counter, he says quietly, "I wrote it."

At least that's what I think he says. I am puzzled. Excuse me?

"I ghost-wrote the book," he says, this time more loudly and definitively. "Cosimo, of course, can barely write a complete sentence. He had the basic idea for the book—it's the story of his kids' hockey team—but he asked me to help him write it. So I did. In fact, I wrote most of it, edited what Cosimo wrote, and

Schreiber, Ontario

worked with the printer to correct the galley proofs." He takes the book and opens it to the dedication and hands it to me. The dedication reads, "To Al Wilson, for his help in making this book a reality."

For a minute I wonder whether Al is delusional, but the more I ponder his revelation, the more I think it might be true. Why else would Cosimo dedicate his one and only book to a man who tends the counter in his gas station? At the same time, given Al's undisguised disdain toward Cosimo, I have to wonder why Al would devote his time and energy to ghostwriting a novel for Cosimo. I can't believe that Cosimo paid him much, if anything. Again it occurs to me that Al might see his mission in life as saving Cosimo from something. But from what? Public embarrassment? Cosimo's own folly? His pride? Something more sinister? I ask him how long he's worked for Cosimo.

Al looks at me for a minute before reluctantly answering, "Fourteen years."

I can't help smiling at him in response, and Al shrugs, as if to say, "I know."

Where do you live? I ask.

"I have a place in the woods near here," he says vaguely.

Al strikes me as an intelligent, well-educated man. Are you from the Schreiber area? I ask.

"No, I spent most of my life in Toronto," he says without elaboration.

What did you do?

"I worked as a manager for Sears and some other large department stores."

He doesn't seem interested in discussing his previous life. With Al certain topics seem to lead nowhere—are conversational cul-de-sacs—while others are on-ramps to the freeway. I want to ask him about his family—whether he has any children and, if so, where they are and what they are doing—but think better of it. Instead I tell him, somewhat blandly, that although I've never visited Toronto, I've heard it's a wonderful city.

He moves his lips soundlessly, moistening his mouth. "It is, or it used to be," he says finally. "But it's changed. There's violent crime now when there never used to be. Nothing like in New York and the other big cities in the States, of course. But Toronto can be a dangerous place. It's beginning to come apart. Like all cities. Like civilization." He pauses and looks me in the eye. "We are nearing the end," he concludes ominously.

I look at him, trying to determine whether he is speaking seriously or ironically. He watches me closely without guile or mirth in his eyes. I say nothing, sensing a psychic precipice.

"If I were you," he says in a confidential whisper. "I'd make plans to get out. Society as we know it is on the verge of collapse." He pauses. "Have you heard of the Illuminati?"

I shake my head.

"The New World Order?"

Again I shake my head.

He studies me for a minute, perhaps considering whether I'm worthy of the information he's about to impart. "They are a group of powerful men," he says then in a quiet, careful voice, "who are working to gain control of the world's financial markets. Do you remember when the American stock market began to free-fall last month? That was a test. They intervened then to halt the slide. But as soon as they have their people in place, they're going to engineer a crash of the world's markets. Then, in the panic that follows, they're going to seize control of the governments of the industrialized nations. In the United

States the Federal Reserve Bank and the Internal Revenue Service are helping them."

He pauses to moisten his lips again before continuing more casually. "My advice to you is to get your money out of the banks and out of the stock market. Invest in precious metals—gold and silver. Buy gold or silver coins—Canadian Maple Leaves, American Eagle dollars, South African Krugerrands. Squirrel them away in your house. If you don't, when you go to the bank to get your money, it won't be there. Trust me, I've done the research."

Pondering his grim prognosis for the world and recalling his computer skills, I ask Al if he does his research on the Internet.

He hesitates for a moment before shaking his head and saying quietly, almost defensively, "Shortwave radio." I nod. I know little about shortwave radio, but I fear that, like many alternative media in our diverse, modern society, it has become the domain primarily of marginal characters—kooks and paranoids. I imagine Al sitting in front of his radio in his secret house in the far North Woods, cocking his head to hear reports of the decline of civilization through a modulating electronic whine.

"And I read," Al continues quickly. "Science and history, mostly. For the past few years I've been working on a big project," he says mysteriously.

I suspect that Al wants me to ask him about his big project, but, right now at least, I don't feel up to the task. My brain is tired, and I'm wary of following him down this particular rabbit hole. As I sit at the counter, he watches me expectantly. For a minute neither of us says anything. Then, unable to restrain himself, Al speaks.

"These are the last days," he says portentously. "We are preparing for an epic battle. The Bible describes it as happening at the place called Armageddon. Revelation, chapter eighteen, verse twenty-one: 'And a mighty angel took up a stone like a great millstone, and cast it into the sea, saying, Thus with violence shall that great city Babylon be thrown down, and shall be found no more at all.'"

* * *

Schreiber may be a "very sound choice as a stopover location" while traveling in the region, as my complimentary visitor map of northwestern Ontario advises, but it is not a place one would choose to stay if one had a reasonable alternative. Except for Rosie and Josie, the restaurants in town are unremarkable; the stores—including Speziale Hardware and Spadoni Department Store—are at best utilitarian; and the lodging options consist of a half-dozen "Canadian motels" (a species long ago identified and described to me by my friend Peter Schultz) laid out along the highway like large, cinder-block coffins.

But in sparsely populated northwestern Ontario, one cannot be too choosy. So Schreiber it is. Now feeling some affiliation with, even allegiance to, the Filane family, I choose Filane's Cosiana Inn for my night's rest. While registering in the motel's cramped, cluttered office, surrounded by more Cosimo Filane merchandise, I chat for a few minutes with Diana Filane. A short, sweet lady with a creamy complexion and straight, shoulder-length, henna-colored hair, Diana has been married to Cosimo for thirty-three years and has borne him eight children. She has a daffy, slightly frazzled air, and I imagine that, after thirty-three years of living with Cosimo, she has earned it. Originally from Cochrane, a remote railroad and timber town located in northeastern Ontario, she comes from an Irish-Canadian family. But now she is the matriarch of Schreiber's most prominent Italian-Canadian family. I suspect that her life has been better than she dared hope for, as a girl growing up in Cochrane.

Indeed, by any standard, the Filane family is, in many ways, exceptional. Domenic, their oldest son, has been the Canadian national light flyweight (106-pound) boxing champion ten times and competed for his country in both the Barcelona and Atlanta Olympic Games. Another son, Gerry, has been the provincial lightweight boxing champion. All the children are involved in some manner in the family's various businesses. Domenic, who recently just missed making the Canadian team for the Sydney Olympic Games, operates a training gym in downtown Schreiber and, in the same building, a retail store called Hollywood Filane Sportswear. Dean, Shawn, and Mario help with marketing and distributing Filane's Canadian Spring Water throughout Ontario, while Edith, the older girl, helps Domenic at the sportswear store, and Deana, the younger one, manages the Can-Op gas station, variety store, and car wash in town. Only one boy, Salvatore, has left the Schreiber area, moving to Toronto, where, in addition to being the marketing rep for the water company, he is pursuing a career as an "entertainer."

Curious about the name "Cosiana" and recalling Cosimo's affinity for contractions, I suddenly have a revelation. I ask Diana about the motel's name.

She laughs good-naturedly. "Oh, it's a combination of Cosimo and Diana," she says, confirming my suspicion. "Most people think my name must be Ana, and I usually don't bother to correct them."

I tell Diana that I'm writing an article about the North Shore of Lake Superior and ask her if Cosimo might be willing to talk to me about life in Schreiber.

She laughs again, something she seems to do easily and often. "Oh, I'm sure he would. I'll see if I can round him up later. Sometimes Cos is hard to catch. He keeps on the move, you know."

* * *

My kitchenette room at the Cosiana Inn is functional, reasonably clean, and remarkably—even spectacularly—ugly. It is furnished 1970s-style with light-brown shag carpet, a chartreuse velour bedspread, and a sleeper sofa with brown plaid upholstery, all of which reek of stale cigarette smoke. (One of the distinguishing characteristics of old-fashioned Canadian motels is that they don't offer nonsmoking rooms.) The kitchenette is minimally equipped with a few mangled utensils and some battle-scarred pots and pans, and the compressor in the refrigerator emits a violent death rattle every time it cycles on. Tonight—a weeknight in the fall—the Cosiana is fully occupied, but Cosimo obviously doesn't like to spend money on unnecessary maintenance or renovation. The carpet and furniture may be the original decor; the walls are bare; and my room contains exactly three working lights: one above the bathroom mirror, a dim overhead light in the kitchen, and a rickety, flickering bedside lamp. The ancient Sony television, however, is connected to a set-top box that brings in more than sixty channels. I may not be able to read in the subterranean light, but I can channel-surf till dawn.

Nevertheless, I feel comfortable in this shabby relic of the 1970s, and it is here, after dinner, that Cosimo visits me. He appears a bit disheveled, his clothes rumpled and his hair—thinner than I remember—tousled and tufted, as if he just arose from a nap. (It reminds me of a bird's crest, after a splash bath.) The top of his shirt is unbuttoned, revealing dark chest hair and a small crucifix pendant, and a pack of cigarettes bulges in his breast pocket. Behind stylish, lightly tinted glasses his eyes look pouchy and tired. Given his large family and diverse business interests, Cosimo's days must be busier and longer than one would expect of someone who lives in a town of eighteen hundred people. (Hearing Cosimo's voice now, I realize that as I was chatting with Diana in the motel's office this afternoon, I overheard him answering a telephone in a back room. "Junior," he exclaimed loudly, "whass happenin'?")

I tell him that I am intrigued by the presence of the Italian-Canadian families in Schreiber.

"Yeah, we have quite a community here. And we're pretty close-knit. Most of the families in town are related by marriage now, so weddings are big affairs. When I was growin' up, it was traditional to marry an Italian girl. But I wanted to be different. I was always kind of rebellious. At first my parents were upset when I decided to marry Di. She's Irish, you know. But that was a long time ago, and now, of course, she's part of the family. We visited relatives in my father's hometown, Siderno, Italy, on our honeymoon.

"We just had a big wedding in the family. Domenic got married this summer to a nice local girl."

His voice is more measured and his affect more subdued than I expected, perhaps because he is tired, perhaps because he knows he is being interviewed and is on his best behavior, trying to make a certain impression.

I ask him if his family speaks Italian at home.

"When I was growing up, we did. My father emigrated from Italy during the Depression, so it was natural for him. But not so much anymore. My mother is still living, and she likes to speak Italian. But my kids, not so much. The old ways are just dying out.

"The young people, they tend to leave the area to look for jobs. There isn't enough excitement for them around here. But I'm lucky. Seven of my eight kids still live here. I have one boy who's in Toronto. He's trying to break into the entertainment business. He sings, and he's appeared in a number of commercials."

I tell Cosimo that he must be proud of his kids' accomplishments.

"Yeah, it's been a good ride. I've been able to travel a lot with Domenic and Gerry when they fight. I went to Barcelona and Atlanta with Domenic, and to Biloxi, Mississippi, when Gerry fought Oscar de la Hoya. They're still young and strong, not like their old man," Cosimo says with a well-practiced, self-deprecating laugh, patting his fleshy middle section. "And the girls have always helped out with the stores."

I tell Cosimo that his family seems to own the entire town.

"Well, when you're in business, you can either try to hide the fact you're in business or you can put your name on everything. You know, get some name recognition. I decided to do that."

He smiles, then says with a chuckle, "A salesman suggested the name 'Fallen Rock' to me. He said that if I called my business 'Fallen Rock,' I'd get free advertising all along the highway from the yellow caution signs that warn of 'fallen rock.'"

He pauses for a few seconds, and his expression turns serious. "I'm just tryin' to make a living for myself and my family," he says in an earnest, almost pious voice that sounds a little too intentional. I feel vaguely as if I'm being fed a line. I can't help thinking that in his younger years Cosimo was a real hellion, slamming down drinks, flirting with the girls, and generally mixing things up at Rocco's Bar.

I also recall that Ned Basher told me that Cosimo, "dressed in a sharkskin suit and looking like a Vegas hustler," has promoted and emceed several "professional" boxing matches in Domenic's gym. However, I sense that Cosimo's budding career as the Don King of the North doesn't jibe with the image he's trying to project tonight—that of a mature patriarch looking out for his family's best interests. So I ask him instead about his singing career.

"Well, I try to keep my hand in. I do the cystic fibrosis telethon in Thunder Bay every year, and I appear in some local clubs. I'm also working on my fifth album with some musicians from Los Angeles. It should be finished soon."

That same information appears on his 1986 novel's dust jacket. His fourth album, "I'm Gonna Try It Again!", appeared in 1983. Cosimo's fifth album is, if nothing else, long awaited.

I mention that I spent some time talking to Al Wilson at the Fallen Rock Can-Op this afternoon and that his employee is quite a character. Cosimo looks down and away, and I can't tell whether he's disappointed that I'm asking about Al or worried about what Al may have told me. He ponders his response for a minute, but when he speaks, all he says is, "Yeah, Al's different, that's for sure."

I don't say anything in response, waiting for Cosimo to elaborate on his relationship with Al, but he just sits quietly, fidgeting in his chair. Finally, to break the silence, I ask him whether he thinks Canadians are different from Americans.

This is more familiar ground, a question many Canadians seem to spend a good deal of time thinking about. "Yeah, I think we are different," he says carefully. "I think Americans are more sure of themselves. More aggressive. Or maybe I should say flamboyant. Americans like to gamble. We Canadians are more reserved, more cautious."

I tell him that to me Canada seems more European, more civilized than the United States. I mention, as an example, national health care.

"Maybe," he concedes, "but Canadians sometimes expect the government to pay for everything. People don't take responsibility for their own lives, and the government has a lot of power. We have too many laws and regulations. It makes it tough to do business. I suppose I'm a conservative, politically speaking. I don't believe in big government."

This topic reminds him of something. "Do you know that Terrace Bay, the town just up the highway, has an ordinance that outlaws smoking at the hospital? Not just inside the building, but on the grounds and in the parking lot. That's crazy! The whole town smells like hell because of the local paper mill, but you can't even smoke a cigarette in the parking lot." He shakes his head.

Having visited Terrace Bay a couple of times previously, I comment that it appears to be a prosperous town.

"Terrace Bay is a newer town, a company town," Cosimo responds, a note of resentment or disdain in his voice. "Kimberly-Clark. You know, the company that makes Kleenex. It doesn't have Schreiber's history. People there come and go."

I get the impression that the two towns don't mix. The hockey games between the high schools must be interesting.

Our conversation seems to be winding down. I ask Cosimo what one or two things a visitor to Schreiber should be sure to see or do.

For a minute the question stumps him, which, perhaps, says more about Schreiber than about Cosimo. Then he has an idea. "There's a little dirt road that follows the railroad tracks west out of town," he says gamely. "You can drive down that road to Schreiber Beach. It's a real pretty little beach located right on the shore of Lake Superior."

* * *

After Cosimo leaves, I get in my car and cruise through a dark and empty downtown Schreiber. Paralleling the railroad tracks, Scotia Street contains all the small-town essentials—municipal office, post office, library, and bank—and it is on Scotia Street that Hollywood Filane Sportswear occupies a two-story, cinder-block building with a handsome facade of carefully fitted sandstone blocks. A blue metal door at one end serves as the entrance to the sportswear store, while a matching door at the other opens into a hallway leading toward the back of the building. A sign over this second door, featuring a stylish red-and-yellow logo of a mountain lion wearing sunglasses and boxing gloves, advertises "Filane's Boxing Team." Parked on the street out front is a late-model Ford Explorer with a vanity license plate reading "Hlywd." Domenic must be at work in the gym.

In the small park with the restored locomotive a plaque memorializes a sad chapter in Canada's modern history:

> During the Second World War, the federal government forcibly evacuated Canadians of Japanese ancestry from the coast of British Columbia. In the spring of 1942, several hundred young men were sent to Ontario to help build the Trans-Canada Highway. They were accommodated in four camps between Schreiber and Jackfish. Most soon left the road camps for work on farms or in lumber and pulp mills. Others, interned in prisoner of war camps for resisting separation from their families, accepted similar employment. Once established in jobs, the men encouraged relatives and friends to migrate east. Thousands settled permanently, establishing the basis of a significant Japanese-Canadian community in Ontario.

Italians in one century, and Japanese-Canadians in the next: the Schreiber area is the empty middle-of-nowhere to which the poor or powerless are dispatched, and where they must carve a living out of the vast and unforgiving taiga.

* * *

The next morning, after eating breakfast in my kitchenette, I pack up and check out of the Cosiana, in the process saying goodbye to Diana and buying from her a CD of Cosimo's 1983 fourth album, "I'm Gonna Try It Again!" (Cosimo co-wrote seven of the eleven tracks, all of which are published by Cosiana Music; the album, marketed by Fallen Rock Productions, includes liner notes by the producer informing me, among other things, that the rhythm section "play[s] regularly on the 'Dukes of Haz[z]ard' T.V. series.") Then, following her directions, I locate a back-alley, basement-level laundromat in downtown Schreiber. There, as I do my week's laundry, I strike up a conversation with the proprietress, Mrs. Krause, who is using most of the machines to wash and dry company-issued jumpsuits for workers at the paper mill in Terrace Bay. The mill is shut down this week for its annual maintenance. It is, she says, her busiest week of the year.

When she finds out I'm from the States, she adopts what I am coming to recognize as Canadians' characteristic attitude toward Americans: respectful, curious, and suspicious. (Canadians generally seem more sensitive than Americans to what they perceive as the significant cultural differences between our two nations.)

Mrs. Krause's elderly mother has been in a hospital in Thunder Bay since recently suffering a heart attack, and Mrs. Krause complains that although her mother is receiving good, free medical care, the government doesn't provide a stipend sufficient to allow family members to stay in a motel near the hospital. Consequently, she has spent many nights sleeping in a chair in her mother's hospital room.

As she speaks, I find myself unexpectedly thinking about Al Wilson, a solitary soul. He's no spring chicken, and when something happens that sends him into the hospital, he too will receive free medical care, but who will keep him company during the night? Cosimo? Perhaps, if Cosimo's familial and other obligations allow. But I worry about Al. His existence is so light, his grip on the planet so tenuous—he might depart this world when no one is looking, might drift away on a breeze, quietly, as on angel wings.

* * *

After finishing my laundry, I drive back west of town to the Fallen Rock Can-Op, where I find Al standing in his customary position behind the counter in the otherwise empty store. It takes him a second to recognize me, but after he does, he almost smiles before asking if I'd like a cup of coffee on the house. I perch on a stool and, after my first taste, compliment him on the coffee, which really is good.

"It's the water. It's good water. Cosimo got lucky with that spring. He doesn't even have to treat it. Just takes it out of the ground and bottles it."

Where is the spring? I ask.

"It's behind the motel. If you walk over there, you'll see it."

I tell him that I stayed at the Cosiana last night and talked to Cosimo in the evening. I mention that Cosimo was more subdued than I expected.

"He may have mellowed a bit over the past few years. He's not as full of bullshit as he once was. I don't let him get away with much around here, and he pretty much leaves me alone. He doesn't cross verbal swords with me," Al says matter-of-factly. Al's comments suddenly cause me to wonder why Cosimo continues to employ him. After fourteen years surely Cosimo is aware of Al's, shall we say, skeptical attitude toward him. Al must provide Cosimo with something Cosimo values. Something other than cheap labor, of which there is no shortage in this part of the world. And something other than Al's asserted writing skills and his practical knowledge about running a business. Does Cosimo—consciously or otherwise—recognize the value of occasionally receiving a reality check from Al? Of occasionally being chastised for his foolish decisions and errant behavior?

As Al and I chat this morning, a burly long-distance trucker stops in for a break, and a few minutes later a young man climbs groggily out of the cab of a Ryder rental truck in the Fallen Rock parking lot and shuffles over. Al pours them cups of coffee, answers their routine questions about this section of the Trans-Canada Highway, and then ignores them. After they leave, he again turns his full attention to me. He seems to have something on his mind.

"Do you remember what we were talking about yesterday?" he asks meaningfully.

I nod, although I'm not sure exactly what he's referring to. We covered a lot of ground in yesterday's conversation.

"Do you read the Bible?"

Probably not as much as I should, I admit.

"The project I'm working on," he says intently, "is interpreting the Bible scientifically, bringing religion and science together." He interlaces the fingers of his two hands in front of him to illustrate the nature of his task. "Reconciling them and discovering the truth common to both . . ."

For the next hour, as Al describes the methodology and results of his research, I concentrate on his words, trying hard to follow his thoughts as they spiral upward. However, although there are moments when the clouds part and I glimpse the firmament, I confess that more often I am lost in the miasma below. Indeed, "bewildered" would not be too strong a term for my state of mind.

What I retain of Al's exposition is this: That we're living in the third of four worlds. The first was destroyed by flood, and the second by ice. And ours will end in fire. All this is as prophesied in the Bible and as described by modern geosciences. For there is scientific evidence, Al tells me, of a global prehistoric flood and, of course, an ice age. And those events are represented as well in the Bible. ("Read the King James version," he advises me. "Forget the Revised Standard.")

There are other parallels between religion and science, Al says. According to the Bible, God created man out of dust and breathed life into him. Recent scientific evidence shows that babies don't exhibit brain waves until birth. A doctor breathing life into a baby therefore is analogous to God breathing life into man. "Dust thou art . . ." (It occurs to me that this information, if true, could be used in a pro-choice argument, though I suspect that Al would bristle at the idea.)

I nod often during our conversation, but, as is often the case, I have trouble grasping the Big Picture. Cosmology, like the unified field theory and international monetary policy, is beyond my ken. As usual, I remain earthbound, rooted to the planet, mired in the present. And so my mind turns to a consideration of some mundane details close at hand: Al's pale blue eyes, his filamentous silver hair, the way the morning light coming through the window haloes his head. After an hour, when Al pauses to catch his breath, I politely excuse myself and walk across the immense gravel parking lot in search of Cosimo's spring.

Schreiber, Ontario

* * *

The ground behind the Fallen Rock Motel slopes down, and the spring and water plant are located literally under the motel, in a cement-floored basement accessible through a garage door that opens to the rear of the building. There, in the basement's damp, chilly atmosphere, Gerry and Dean Filane and a middle-aged man named Rick disinfect clear-plastic five-gallon containers, fill them with water straight out of a hose, and use a forklift to load pallets of the containers onto the company's delivery trucks. The men work steadily, but Rick, at least, seems happy for some company.

Rick is trim and fit, with lively blue eyes and long gray hair tied in a ponytail that streams down his back from beneath the dam of his baseball cap. Rick has worked for Cosimo for about five years and has the distinction of being the only employee of Filane's Canadian Spring Water who is not a member of the Filane family. Originally from Toronto, he moved to Thunder Bay in the late 1970s before marrying a woman from Schreiber and relocating here. Rick is a classic North Woods outdoorsman: he enjoys hunting, fishing, snowmobiling, and, he adds with a sheepish grin, "drinkin' a beer or two now and then."

Filane's Canadian Spring Water is distributed throughout most of Ontario. Dean delivers to the bush towns north of Schreiber, while Gerry handles the route along the northern shore of Lake Superior west to Thunder Bay and east toward Sault Sainte Marie. As I watch Rick and the boys work, it occurs to me that the water may be free, but that, because of its volume and weight, the labor and transportation costs associated with its distribution are considerable. Water weighs about eight pounds per gallon, and I'm suddenly glad I'm not schlepping hundreds of containers weighing forty pounds each around northwestern Ontario. The water retails for about seven Canadian dollars per container, and I wonder, after expenses, how much money Cosimo actually makes from this enterprise, given the product's limited distribution.

I ask Rick if they treat the water, and he says they don't need to, that it comes out of the well pipe cold and pure. Then, lowering his voice and glancing around nervously, he mentions that Cosimo has more than once attracted the attention of the provincial public-health authorities by not submitting required water samples on time.

At one point during the morning Domenic stops by. He is short and compact, all muscle and sinew, and he moves with leonine grace and efficiency. As he talks with his brothers, they tease him good-naturedly about the changes his recent marriage will work on his bachelor lifestyle and Olympian physique.

Finally, as I am preparing to leave, Cosimo himself appears. He acts surprised and, I think, a little disconcerted to see me here. I may be getting into his business more than he would like. He is wearing a nylon-shelled jacket with the water company's logo on the back and, as seems to be his habit, tinted glasses. He fidgets with a lit cigarette as he observes the loading operation. If anything, he looks slightly more disheveled than last night, and I find myself wondering what he did after he left my room at the Cosiana.

I tell him that water may be his ticket to the big time, that people these days will pay top dollar for good-tasting, pure, "natural" water.

"Maybe," he replies. "I'm talking to some people about investing some money in the company so that we can upgrade our distribution network. I thought I had a deal with one gentleman from the States, but he just backed out."

I ask him how much money he's talking about.

Cosimo ponders his response for a minute. Maybe he thinks I'm a potential investor. "Oh, about ten thousand dollars," he says carefully.

Ten thousand dollars is nothing, I think. Venture capitalists spend that much money on lunches in five-star restaurants. Cosimo should think bigger. But I don't have ten thousand dollars in my bank account and Cosimo's business is his business, so I keep my thoughts to myself.

Cosimo, I tell him instead, you could be rich.

He studies me for a minute, his guard still up. "I'm not lookin' to be rich," he says in his earnest voice. "I'm just tryin' to support my family."

* * *

Later in the afternoon, as I drive west toward Nipigon and Thunder Bay through the somber hills and dark boreal forest of the Canadian Shield—through that primordial landscape—I think about Cosimo and his industrious family. People of apparently boundless energy, they are the preeminent—or at least the most visible—entrepreneurs in this isolated corner of Canada. By dint of their hard work and sheer number, they are uncommonly successful, making a comfortable living in a part of the world that no one has ever found hospitable. And they do it without getting their hands dirty, as the saying goes.

Cosimo himself seems a figure in transition. I have no doubt that as a young man he was, in both his personal and professional lives, a veritable Vesuvius of schemes, lines, deals, come-ons, and trade-offs. (As Al would say, bullshit.) Now, well into middle age, he seems to be in the process of diminishing his expectations and reinventing himself as the august patriarch of his clan. Nevertheless, beneath the veneer of manners and maturity, one can still detect his youthful vitality, ambition, and chutzpah.

But of course I can't think about Cosimo without also thinking about his employee, associate, conscience, and nemesis, Al Wilson. Like a watchful raven, Al circles over Cosimo's life, cawing his criticism. He might be Cosimo's guardian angel or avenging angel—I'm not sure which. And perhaps for that reason I can't imagine one without the other. Isolated in the hinterlands of northwestern Ontario, locked in free-falling conflict and embrace, they are coupled in my mind like Grant and Lee, Ali and Frazier, Laurel and Hardy.

As I leave Schreiber farther behind, I slip my new CD into the car's player and listen as Cosimo, backed by a small orchestra with a Big Band sound, sings one of his original compositions. The slow-swinging melody is reminiscent of "New York, New York," and Cosimo's phrasing is positively Sinatraesque:

> I'm gonna try it again.
> I'm gonna give it my best shot.
> I'll try to make it again.
> This time I'll shoot right for the top.
> And when I rise,
> I won't be standin' alone,
> I'll see your smilin' face,
> With that funny grin,
> The one that set me out to win.

Now my love's here to stay.
I'll turn the night right into day.
I'll be the best on the vine,
The finest vintage of the wine.
I'm gonna deal in happiness.
I'll show the world what love can do.
For you, I'm gonna try it again,
Again and again,
Again and again,
Again and again,
Again and again.

Diminuendo.

# # #

Sault Sainte Marie, Ontario and Michigan: The Synergy of Place

We came after to a rapid that makes the separation of the lake of the hurrons, that we calle Superior, or upper. . . . Wee made cottages att our advantages, and found the truth of what those men [Indian guides] had often [said], that if once we could come to that place we should make good cheare of a fish that they call *Assickmack*, which signifieth a white fish. The bear, the castors [beavers], and the Oriniack [moose] shewed themselves often, but to their cost; indeed it was to us like a terrestriall paradise.

Peter Esprit Radisson, *Voyages of Peter Esprit Radisson, Being an Account of his Travels and Experiences Among the North American Indians, from 1652 to 1684*

Today the broad, braided, sixty-mile-long water passage between Lake Superior and Lake Huron is called the Saint Mary's River. Over that distance the river falls a total of about twenty-five feet, most of the drop occurring in a series of rapids located near the outlet from the upper lake. *Saut* meant "river rapid" in archaic French; thus, according to most historians, early French missionaries, honoring the Virgin Mary, named the area Saut de Sainte Marie. The modern city of Sault Sainte Marie, Ontario, and its smaller American counterpart, Sault Sainte Marie, Michigan, are located on opposite sides of these rapids. In addition to the names, the local French pronunciation has stuck; on both sides of the international border the cities are still referred to simply as "the Soo."

All the surface water leaving Lake Superior funnels through the Saint Mary's River, flowing at an average rate of seventy-eight thousand cubic feet per second. That is a huge amount of water, more than fifty *billion* gallons per day, enough to meet the drinking, cooking, and bathing needs of every human now living on the planet, if only it were economical to capture, transport, and distribute it.

Bands of Chippewa or Ojibwe Indians traditionally hunted, fished, and camped near the Saint Mary's rapids, where game and fish abounded. (The Indians known historically in the United States as the Chippewas were more commonly known in Canada as the Ojibwas or Ojibwes, which is the term most tribal members prefer today. The Ojibwes are culturally and linguistically related to other tribes in the Great Lakes region, who refer to themselves collectively as *Anishinaabe*.) At the time of European contact the Ojibwes were the dominant tribe in the upper Great Lakes—in 1661 they repelled a large Iroquois war party along the southeastern shore of Lake Superior, and by the early nineteenth century, as a result of long, intermittent warfare, they had displaced the Dakota (Sioux) to west of the Mississippi River—and Sault Sainte Marie was one of their favored gathering places.

Sault Sainte Marie also figured prominently in the European colonization of the upper Great Lakes. In 1668 Père Jacques Marquette, the intrepid Jesuit priest, established a mission on the southwestern side of the rapids. Then, on June 14, 1671, a young French military officer, Simon-François Daumont de Saint-Lusson, formally took possession of the interior of North America for King Louis XIV in a ceremony at Sault Sainte Marie attended by representatives of the local Indian tribes. After emerging from the palisaded mission in a procession of French priests and traders and bestowing gifts on the assembled Indians, Daumont de Saint-Lusson recited three times the elaborate language of possession, claiming for France the immediate area and then, expansively, "Lakes Superior and Huron, the Island of Manitoulin and all the other countries, rivers, lakes, and streams contiguous and adjacent thereunto: both those which have been discovered and those which may be discovered hereafter, in all their length and breadth, bounded on the one side by the seas of the North and of the West, and on the other by the South Sea. . . ." After he finished, the Frenchmen shouted "Vive le roi!"; the traders fired their muskets into the air; and the tribal representatives signed a record of the proceedings, ostensibly acknowledging their subservience to the distant Sun King.

Sault Sainte Marie remained under French control until the conclusion of the French and Indian War in 1763, when France ceded virtually all its North American possessions to Great Britain through what is known as the Treaty of Paris

(1763). Twenty years later representatives of the newly formed United States and of Great Britain concluded the American Revolution by signing the Definitive Treaty of Peace, also known (confusingly) as the Treaty of Paris (1783), which described the boundary between the United States and the remaining British possessions in North America as following the "water-communication" between Lakes Huron and Superior, i.e., the Saint Mary's River. During the War of 1812 the Americans captured the portion of Sault Sainte Marie lying north of the river because of its strategic importance but relinquished it through the Treaty of Ghent (1814), which concluded *that* war.

Thus for hundreds of years Sault Sainte Marie has been a center of human population and a locus of human activity in the upper Great Lakes. People have been drawn to this place as if by a strange magnetism in the rocks. But the Saint Mary's River itself may provide the best metaphor for what has happened here: the steady current of trade and commerce; the swirling, sometimes turbulent mix of races and cultures; the treacherous shoals of politics and war; and, occasionally, deep, still pools of religious faith.

* * *

The early October rain is unrelenting. For five days I have been visiting the Sault Sainte Marie area; for five days the air has been saturated with moisture, the sky has been leaden, and the temperature has hovered between 35°F and 45°F. I had intended to camp for at least part of my time here, but the weather has sent me scurrying for cover, and I have burrowed into the Glenview Vacation Cottages a few miles north of town.

The cottages are pleasant modern units set off the Trans-Canada Highway in a mixed stand of evergreen and deciduous trees, and here I read, cook my meals, take short walks through the sodden forest, and occasionally venture into the city. And here, in the evenings, watch cable television, especially the Weather Channel—I said the cottages were pleasant, not rustic—which for five days now has shown a massive, stationary low-pressure system sitting over northern Ontario, southwest of James Bay. The counter-clockwise flow around the low repeatedly spins storms and squalls off Lake Superior, inundating the countryside. During the past five days I have seen the sun for a total of two or three hours.

I am beginning to appreciate where all the water flowing down the Saint Mary's River comes from. The Lake Superior basin is relatively small, encompassing an area of land only one and a half times the area of the lake itself, but it receives an average of about thirty inches of precipitation annually—including as much as 150 inches of snow in the lake-effect belt along the lake's southern and eastern shores. Because only about six hundred thousand people live in the entire basin and because the basin supports little agriculture, the amount of water consumed by human activity is relatively small. Although a surprising amount of water evaporates from the lake's surface each year—some scientists estimate as much as 40 percent of the lake's total inflow—the remainder leaves the lake through the Saint Mary's River.

I am also beginning to appreciate why this part of Canada is, even today, relatively unpopulated. Despite the abundance of natural resources—water, fish, wildlife, timber, and minerals—it is an inhospitable place. Several days ago, as I drove from Marathon to Sault Sainte Marie, a distance of about 260 miles, I passed myriad lakes, wetlands, and bogs; countless streams and rivers; and vast stands of boreal forest; but only a couple of permanent towns—White River and Wawa—and a handful of summer-seasonal communities along the shore of Lake Superior. In the car the cold rain splattered on the windshield, the tires hissed quietly on the wet pavement, and I listened to a series of pieces by the Finnish composer Jean Sibelius—"En Saga," "Tapiola," and "The Oceanides"—austere, beautiful music that seemed particularly suited to this empty northern landscape. The solitude, scenery, weather, and music combined to draw me into a pensive mood, and for a couple of hours I imagined myself cast off in this wilderness with only what I could carry on my back, stripped of the protective armor of modern technology and forced to fend for myself. Although I am fit, in good health, and pride myself on being a competent outdoorsman, I found myself seriously questioning my ability to survive for more than, say, a few days. Here in the northern forest misfortune and death could befall a person in many ways: hypothermia, malnutrition, disease, drowning, an accidental fall, a large-animal attack. I thought about Chris McCandless, the young man whose journey to, and demise in, the Alaskan wilderness was the subject of Jon Krakauer's book *Into the Wild*; about the narrow range of environmental conditions in which we humans evolved and still feel comfortable; about the fragility of our species. Despite the beauty of the landscape, it was a sobering, even melancholy drive.

* * *

Sault Sainte Marie is famous, of course, for its canals and locks. Before they were constructed, all cargo transported up or down the Saint Mary's River had to be hauled around the rapids. In 1797-98 the North West Company constructed the first canal around the rapids; it reportedly had a depth of about two feet and was suitable only for canoes. The Americans destroyed it when they captured Sault Sainte Marie in the War of 1812. After the war the United States Army constructed a canal for canoe passage on the American side of the rapids. Then in 1855 the State of Michigan constructed the first lock system on the American side. The state subsequently enlarged the locks to accommodate the increasing ship traffic on Lake Superior and in 1881 transferred them to the federal government, which also enlarged them and continues to operate them through the United States Army Corps of Engineers. In 1895 the Canadians completed a lock system on their side of the channel, but it soon proved inadequate for the progressively larger cargo ships plying the Great Lakes, and in 1979 the Canadian government formally retired it from the Saint Lawrence Seaway. Today a smaller, reconstructed lock, administered as part of Canada's Sault Canal National Historic Site, is used only by recreational and tour boats. The Soo locks are still impressively busy: each year about ten thousand vessels, about half of them large cargo ships, pass through the American side.

One afternoon I drive into Sault Sainte Marie, plunk down twenty bucks, and take a guided boat tour of the locks. Competing American and Canadian companies conduct the tours from terminals on opposite sides of the river. Curious about the Canadian spin on the area's history, I opt for the Canadian version, on a stout seventy-foot-long double-decker boat named the Chief Shingwauk, after a prominent local Ojibwe chief who was loyal to King George III and who fought against the Americans in the War of 1812. The Chief Shingwauk is capable of carrying two hundred passengers; on this damp, gray, blustery day, however, only about ten of us think that being on the water is a good idea, and we disperse ourselves casually around the enclosed, heated lower deck as, during the two-hour tour, a crew member reads a carefully worded script over a loudspeaker.

The Chief Shingwauk joins its American counterpart on the far side of the channel, and the two boats follow the same route, first being lifted upriver in the smallest American lock as an enormous cargo ship sailing under Hong Kong registry utilizes the adjacent larger one. The sight of a thousand-foot-long oceangoing cargo ship rising effortlessly on a controlled, contained tide of fresh water is remarkable, even eerie. The whole process is nearly silent, which only adds to the impression that we are witnessing something that contravenes the physical laws that normally govern our world.

After exiting the lock, the tour boats continue upriver, passing far beneath the 2.8-mile-long international highway bridge before turning toward the Canadian shore. From midriver we have a good view downstream of the Saint Mary's rapids, braided into channels by cobbled, willow-fringed islands. Water flows into the channels like dark molten glass, then breaks over the submerged rocks like delicate crystal. Although the river's volume has been significantly reduced by diversions for the locks and canals and a hydroelectric plant on the American shore, paddling a canoe through the rapids would still be a hazardous endeavor. A single mistake could capsize the craft, throwing the occupants into the icy, fast-moving water and forcing them to struggle frantically to shore before exhaustion or hypothermia ended the game. Historian Grace Lee Nute reports that in the eighteenth and early nineteenth centuries "it was considered *de rigueur* for every traveler to the Sault to descend the rapids in a canoe." People, I think, were tougher then, more accustomed to physical hardship and risk; and although part of me longs for such challenges and excitement, at the same time I'm thankful for the modern comforts and safety of the Chief Shingwauk.

The boats then tour the Canadian shoreline, providing close-up views of the Algoma Steel Mill, Sault Sainte Marie's largest employer, and the Saint Mary's Forest Products Company plant. Like all the cities around Lake Superior, Sault Sainte Marie is a working-class town. Although strips of chain motels, restaurants, and gift shops catering to the tourist trade are developing along the Trans-Canada Highway north of the city and along the riverfront near the international bridge, its bread and butter remains the steel and paper mills. In old downtown Sault Sainte Marie, along Queen and Wellington Streets, one is struck by the practical nature of the storefront businesses—food markets, drug stores, and five-and-dimes— and the shoppers' purposeful strides. If one wants a cup of coffee here, one does not look for a Starbuck's.

The boats finally lock down through the reconstructed Canadian canal before concluding the tour with a brief look at the American and Canadian shores below the terminals. On this part of the trip one sees and appreciates the unreduced flow of the Saint Mary's River, which swells to nearly a mile across, lapping at its banks. (If the water were warmer, a strong swimmer might be able, with some effort, to cross the river; the temperature of the water, however, renders that feat superhuman.) As in many other places around Lake Superior, the world here is a wash of blues and greens: the eggshell sky (occasionally visible through broken gray clouds), the ultramarine water, the verdant islands and banks. When I step outside onto the foredeck, the breeze is moist and bracing but without the briny smell, which, having grown up near the ocean, I expect around large bodies of water. The spray that occasionally splatters my glasses dries without leaving any salt residue, and the atmosphere is aqueous, pure, and heady—a natural, cleansing aerosol.

* * *

The next day, as the rain continues to fall, I plunk down considerably more than twenty bucks to ride the Agawa Canyon train. The train is operated by the Algoma Central Railway and runs on tracks that were laid in the early years of the twentieth century from Sault Sainte Marie to Hearst, Ontario, about three hundred miles north. The impetus for the railroad's construction, of course, was commercial: to provide a means of transporting iron ore, copper, and timber out of that remote and largely inaccessible area. (The railway company had originally intended to lay the tracks all the way to Hudson Bay but abandoned those ambitious plans because of the difficulty and expense of construction.) Although the railway company still uses the tracks to transport timber out of the forest, today it also uses them to operate a seasonal passenger train for tourists, offering daily round-trip excursions from Sault Sainte Marie to Agawa Canyon, 114 rail-miles north, and providing access to hunting and fishing camps and lodges deep in the northern forest.

"Algoma" is the name not only of the railway company but also of this region of Ontario. Although vaguely Indian-sounding, the word was invented by Henry R. Schoolcraft, a prominent white American who lived in Sault Sainte Marie and served as the Indian agent for northern Michigan and Wisconsin from 1822 to 1841. During that time he married a local woman whose mother was a full-blooded Ojibwe Indian and whose grandfather had been an Ojibwe headman or chief; became a dedicated student of Indian culture; and wrote numerous books about the Algonquin-speaking tribes of the upper Great Lakes, including one bearing the quaint title *The Indian in his Wigwam: Characteristics of the Red Race of America from Original Notes and Manuscripts*. His work, well known in his own day, inspired Henry Wadsworth Longfellow to write "The Song of Hiawatha."

The Agawa Canyon train, which bills itself as "a journey into the Canadian wilderness," is popular with tourists from the American Midwest, and it is quite a production, particularly during the busy fall color season. Today, for example, the train includes sixteen passenger coaches, together seating more than a thousand paying customers, and a couple of dining cars. On this weekday in early October the crowd is an older one; about half the people in my coach are members of a group of retirees from Madison, Wisconsin. Most of the passengers also appear— how can I put this delicately?—well fed. Based on this admittedly skewed sample of the population, we middle-aged and older Americans tend to be a hefty lot. A man who worked for the railway company in its early years noted wryly, "At the start of any trip from the Sault, the female passengers were isolated (barricaded) in a separate coach at the rear of the train while the front coaches were filled with uneven-tempered lumberjacks. This arrangement offered a modicum of protection for the members of the delicate sex as the only males they had to fight off were the members of the train crew and the traveling clergy . . ." A hundred years later the tables have turned. At least on this particular day the train's clientele is overwhelmingly female, and those who still have husbands lead their docile, stiff-legged men up and down the train's aisles as if by their noses.

The train winds its way slowly north through a rolling landscape known as the Chapleau Uplands, gradually climbing at an average speed of about thirty miles per hour. We pass one lake after another, a cool breeze ruffling their dark surfaces like a loon's feathers, and cross numerous streams and rivers, all flowing west toward Lake Superior. The high steel trestles over the larger watercourses—particularly the Montreal River, where we overlook a massive hydroelectric dam—are vertiginous. The forest is a mix of evergreen and deciduous trees, and even on a gray, rainy day the sugar maples are explosive, the aspens and birches incandescent. The true boreal forest, located farther north, is a dark, monochromatic place, dominated by large, unbroken stands of balsam fir, black and white spruce, and tamarack. I recall hearing that maples and most other deciduous trees cannot survive sustained winter temperatures below -40°F and that that isotherm marks the southern edge of the boreal forest. On this trip we will approach but not cross that boundary.

The train's destination is Agawa Canyon, a 575-foot-deep cleft in the earth, widened and rounded by glacial action, with forested slopes and pink granite cliffs and outcrops over which several tributary streams cascade toward the Agawa River. From Mile 97, the summit of the line (about a thousand vertical feet above Sault Sainte Marie), the train descends over the next seventeen miles to the canyon's floor, where the railway company has developed a private "wilderness park," including a food concession, a vintage train car that has been converted to a souvenir shop, and a well-maintained trail system. The company claims that the park is capable of accommodating a hundred thousand visitors per year, but a thousand people arriving on a single train for a two-hour layover makes the place feel crowded. I sometimes think that there are two kinds of people in the world: those who fear solitude and silence—essential components of a wilderness experience—and arrange their lives to avoid them, and those who seek them out, at least occasionally, to quiet their minds and to acknowledge and appreciate something outside of, and greater than, themselves. In a light, intermittent rain I dutifully tour the canyon, sharing the trails and lookouts with various groups of people who seem to talk constantly, their words and breath condensing in the cool air and forming an opaque fog that obscures the world around them. Although the canyon is lovely, visiting it with a thousand other tourists is hardly a wilderness experience.

On the long ride back to the Soo I stare out the window at the kaleidoscope of colors sliding by the windows. I recall a line from an old Jim Harrison essay: "[I]n Canada is this sense of something we have largely lost." That is still true. Lulled by the train's motion and the tired, muted conversations of my fellow travelers, I doze and dream of a time when the forest through which we effortlessly glide was a place of hardship, danger, silence, and stealth.

* * *

Today almost half Sault Sainte Marie's population of eighty-five thousand people is Catholic, one of the enduring legacies of the Jesuits' presence in this part of the New World. During the period when the French and the English competed for control of North America, the Society of Jesus dispatched hundreds of young priests to the gloomy, frigid wilderness of New France with two complementary goals: to convert the heathen tribes to Christianity and to secure their allegiance to the mother country. The Jesuits kept detailed records of their activities in New France, collected annually in volumes known as the *Relations*, and many historians, notably Francis Parkman, have recognized the priests' importance in North America's history. (Parkman devoted an entire volume of his magisterial seven-volume work, *France and England in North America*, to the Jesuits' influence.) The stories of their labors among the Hurons, in the years before the Iroquois decimated their linguistic cousins, are near-mythic tales of struggle, hardship, and, for some, martyrdom. (*Black Robe*, a 1991 film directed by Bruce Beresford, depicts, in haunting beauty and gruesome detail, the journey of a young Jesuit priest to the Huron mission.)

The most famous Jesuit of this era, at least in the United States, was Jacques Marquette. Born in 1637 in Laon, in northern France, Marquette had become a priest by the age of seventeen. In 1666 he was assigned to New France, where, two years later, he established the fledgling mission at Sault Sainte Marie. He then journeyed farther into the wilderness to La Pointe, near the western end of Lake Superior, to another recently established mission. He stayed at La Pointe for two years, ministering to the Ottawas and a few surviving Hurons, all refugees from the fearsome and bellicose Iroquois to the east. La Pointe was a gathering place for many tribes, and during Marquette's time there he heard from the Illinois Indians of a great river they crossed on their annual visits. He came to believe that this river flowed into the Gulf of California, and his desire grew to explore it and to proselytize to the Indians living in the villages along its banks. In the summer of 1671, however, Marquette and his charges were forced to flee eastward to escape the enmity of the Sioux (whom the Jesuits called "the Iroquois of the west"). They finally settled at Point Saint Ignace, on the shore of Lake Huron north of the Straits of Mackinac, where Marquette established yet another mission.

By all accounts Marquette was a devout, steadfast, and quietly formidable man. In his characteristic style, both authoritative and vivid, Parkman described the Jesuit's character thus: "The longings of a sensitive heart, divorced from earth, sought solace in the skies. A subtile element of romance was blended with the fervor of his worship, and hung like an illumined cloud over the harsh and hard realities of his daily lot. Kindled by the smile of his celestial mistress [the Virgin Mary], his gentle and noble nature knew no fear. For her he burned to dare and to suffer, discover new lands and conquer new realms to her sway."

So it was that Marquette was honored and excited when the governor of New France appointed him to accompany Louis Jolliet, a Québec-born priest-turned-fur-trader, on an expedition to explore the Mississippi River. On May 17, 1673, the two men embarked from Saint Ignace in two canoes with five voyageurs of mixed French and Indian blood. They paddled through the Straits of Mackinac, along the northern shore of Lake Michigan, up Green Bay and into the Fox River, across Lake Winnebago, and up the meandering river beyond, choked with wild rice. Then, after a mile-and-a-half-long marshy portage, they launched onto the Wisconsin River, a tributary of the Mississippi. They glided downstream, reaching the river's confluence with the Father of Waters near the site of present-day Prairie du Chien, Wisconsin. The small group then floated and sailed downstream on the Mississippi, observing moose and buffalo along the banks; sighting on a distant bluff a large red, black, and green pictograph of a grotesque anthropomorphous figure, which Marquette thought demonic; experiencing the outflow of the Missouri River in flood; and eventually, after a tense meeting, feasting with bands of Indians near the mouth of the Arkansas River. Realizing at this point that the Mississippi flowed into the Gulf of Mexico, not the Gulf of California, and worried about encountering hostile Spaniards and Indians farther south, Marquette and Jolliet reversed course and began the long, arduous trip upstream. They finally reached Green Bay at the end of September, after a four-month absence and a journey of more than twenty-five hundred miles. The indefatigable Jolliet continued to Québec to report to the governor, while Marquette remained at the Jesuit mission on Green Bay, afflicted with dysentery.

A year later, still suffering from his malady, Marquette embarked from Green Bay with the intention of founding a new mission among the Illinois Indians. He and his two guides paddled along the western shore of Lake Michigan and over-wintered along the Chicago River before resuming their journey to the large Indian town called Kaskaskia, on the Illinois River. Arriving there in March, he was received "like an angel from Heaven." Although weak, Marquette found the strength to instruct the assembled Indians on the tenets and mysteries of the faith. Then, a few days after Easter, he and his guides departed, intending to return to Saint Ignace.

As they were paddling along the eastern shore of Lake Michigan, however, Marquette's health declined. He asked his guides to carry him to a rise of land on the banks of a small tributary river, where he asked their forgiveness for causing them so much trouble, heard their confessions, and gave them directions for his burial. He died that night, at the age of thirty-eight, murmuring the names of Jesus and Mary. Two years later a party of Ottawa Indians, whom Marquette had instructed at La Pointe, found his grave, exhumed his skeleton, and, in Parkman's words, "washed and dried the bones and placed them carefully in a box of birchbark. Then, in a procession of thirty canoes, they bore it, singing their funeral songs, to St. Ignace of Michillimackinac."

On my last full day in the Sault Sainte Marie area I drive an hour south to Saint Ignace, Michigan, to pay my respects to the great Jesuit priest. As I drive, I evidently pass out of the low-pressure system's circulation, for the weather improves markedly. Here, on the shores of Lake Huron, shafts of sunlight pierce the clouds, and the rain is only showery. I visit the former Saint Ignace Mission chapel, now a museum of Ojibwe Indian culture, on whose grounds Marquette's remains were re-interred. Then I ride one of the high-speed commercial ferries to Mackinac Island, where I walk through the carefully maintained Victorian village (crowded with fudge shops, antique stores, and bundled tourists) to see the imposing bronze statue of Marquette in a small state park. From a hill I can see the Mackinac Bridge over the white-capped straits. The wind off the water is bracing, and I imagine the saintly priest, the faithful trapper, and their small party rounding the point in their canoes, paddling steadily into the gale, heading resolutely into the unknown interior of the continent.

* * *

For my last night in the Sault Sainte Marie area I splurge and move into town to the Brockwell Chambers, a bed-and-breakfast operated by Maria Sutton, a Dutch woman now married to a retired Canadian forester. Five years ago, when I arrived in town on a weekend in late September without a hotel reservation and discovered how crowded the Soo can be during the fall color season, Maria saved me from an uncertain night when she had a last-minute cancellation. She is a lovely woman and gracious hostess, with a smile as radiant as the Northern Lights, and I feel lucky to be able to spend another night in her comfortable home.

At breakfast the next morning, as Maria quietly serves and clears dishes, I strike up a conversation with a middle-aged couple, dressed in smart casual attire, sitting at the next table. The man—I'll call him Gerald—has a handsome face with well-formed features and a burnished complexion, and his silver-rimmed glasses rims match his neatly trimmed hair. His manner is reserved and proper—studious, even—and when he speaks, which is only occasionally, he does so in precise, clipped sentences. The woman—let's call her Ruth—is paler than her husband, with a fuller face. Her appearance, like his, is quite proper—her mouse-colored hair is fixed in a beauty-shop wave and her blouse is buttoned to the neck—but she is chattier and less circumspect than he. They live in the town of Niagara-on-the-Lake in southeastern Ontario and have driven to the Sault Sainte Marie area to see the fall colors and ride the Agawa Canyon train. They then plan to cross the border into the United States to tour Mackinac Island and visit some of Ruth's relatives in the Detroit area before circling home.

Gerald is in charge of operations for the Saint Lawrence Seaway, which, he explains, has been "commercialized"—privatized—in recent years. Although the Canadian government continues to own the seaway's infrastructure, in 1998 it transferred all the system's personal property and responsibility for its operations to a nonprofit corporation that is expected to become self-supporting through the collection of fees from ships using the Canadian canals and locks. (Gerald makes a point of telling me that although the United States doesn't charge for the use of its canals and locks, it more than makes up for it by charging hefty port fees.) Ruth is a realty specialist with the Ontario provincial government, a dull-sounding job that she describes with surprising enthusiasm.

For a time our conversation consists of meaningless chitchat. Ruth complains about the service and noise at a nearby upscale restaurant where she and Gerald ate dinner a couple of nights earlier, and we commiserate with each other about the dismal weather, particularly when the rain outside the window turns to wet snow. ("Oh no, it's too early," Ruth exclaims several times. "I'm not ready!") They assure me that the climate in southeastern Ontario is mild compared to that in Sault Sainte Marie.

"We live in the Banana Belt of Canada," Ruth says cheerfully. "There are vineyards everywhere—it's becoming quite a renowned wine-making region—and even peach trees." As she eagerly describes the virtues of home, Gerald sits quietly, his expression composed and neutral.

Despite the assertedly benign climate of southeastern Ontario, they are beginning to look for a part-time retirement locale where they can escape the Canadian winters for two or three months each year. In their search they have traveled to southern Europe, Mexico, Florida, and Arizona, and this coming year they plan to spend a month in Spain and Portugal. ("I love sherries and ports," Ruth confides with a laugh.)

Eventually, however, as we linger at our tables, the talk turns to current affairs and politics, and Gerald suddenly takes a more active role in the conversation. I am surprised by the quiet vehemence with which he takes the United States to task for, among other things, its recent invasion and occupation of Iraq and its longstanding embargo of Cuba.

"We've been to Cuba, and so have many of our friends," Gerald says carefully, controlling the emotion in his voice. "Some Canadians own a resort hotel a couple of hours east of Havana. They hire only the local villagers to work there, and they treat them very well. The employees accrue credits based on the number of year they've worked there, and after so many years the hotel pays for them to travel anywhere in the world. It may sound incredible, but it's true. Anyway, we stayed at the hotel, and we took down a care package, which the hotel distributes to local families. Just some necessities and a few presents for the children—toothbrushes, stuffed animals, things like that. They need everything. The United States' embargo is simply inhumane. I don't understand why your government insists on doing it."

I nod. I silently agree with him, but I feel unsure how to respond. I love my country, but my feelings about it are complicated. Nonetheless, I am reluctant to criticize it in front of someone I have just met. To do so would feel . . . cheap, like complaining about your marriage to a stranger in a bar. Moreover, I don't feel competent to engage in a serious discussion about America's foreign policies. So in response I offer only the bland observation that the last fifty years of American-Cuban relations have not exactly been rational.

Gerald seems to understand, and he is too well mannered to pursue the subject and spoil our conversation. So we return to safer topics. I tell them that I think they will enjoy Mackinac Island, which is, by any standard, a beautiful place. Ruth says she has wanted to visit it since she saw *Somewhere in Time*, a

1980 movie starring Christopher Reeve and Jane Seymour that was filmed on the island and showcased the magnificent Grand Hotel. The movie, a romantic fantasy, was not to my taste, but I say nothing to Ruth, who seems enthralled by its memory and excited by the prospect of visiting its location.

* * *

I suppose that borders are, by definition, edgy places—zones of heightened activity, awareness, and nervous energy. That principle seems to operate on many levels. In an ecosystem, individuals of the same species who occupy different habitats may encounter each other along the border of their ranges; the result may be a lethal struggle for dominance or a sudden coupling, producing offspring of hybrid vigor. And the border between two modern nations often marks (and, over time, emphasizes) differences in ethnicity, language, custom, politics, and law—everything that anthropologists refer to as "culture." People look, talk, and act differently "over there," and an activity or product legal in one country may be illicit in the other. Where different cultures touch or mingle, they create a world that is exciting, often tawdry, and sometimes even dangerous. The combination is alluring; we are drawn to it almost as much as we are drawn to the familiar faces of home.

Although we usually think of Canada and Canadians as refined and restrained, even Sault Sainte Marie partakes of some of the tawdriness of border towns. Colorful billboards around the city advertise Studio 10, a strip club featuring "exotic dancers" that is co-located with a hotel of questionable propriety on a back street near the international bridge. (Its website, according to the billboards, is www.kinky-studio.com.) And on a previous visit to the city I observed an altercation in a downtown parking lot between a motel manager, a disheveled guest, and a drunken woman who was apparently a familiar local prostitute.

"Get out of here," the manager yelled as he shooed the stumbling woman across the lot and the guest retreated toward his motel room's open door. "I told you never to come back, or I'd call the police."

In this era of global conflict and terrorist threat, the border crossing between the United States and Canada is not the mere formality it was only a few years ago. So I have tried to prepare myself for this portion of the trip. I have brought my recently renewed passport and other forms of identification; I have told myself to answer the customs officer's questions simply and directly (and not ironically or ambiguously, as I am sometimes inclined to do); and I have picked a slow time— midmorning on a weekday—to cross back into the United States. But my karma at borders has always been bad . . .

Customs and Border Protection, an agency of the United States Department of Homeland Security, is enlarging and upgrading the port of entry at Sault Sainte Marie, Michigan, using funds appropriated by Congress for the "war against terrorism." But on this slow morning the old port, dividing noncommercial traffic into just two lanes, is more than adequate. When I reach the crossing, after waiting only a couple of minutes for the vehicles ahead of mine to clear, I hand the customs officer my passport, and he asks me where I'm from. When I say New Mexico, he pauses and steps out of his booth to check my car's license plates: Minnesota. I sense that I am already in a different category than I wanted to be.

"Is that a rental car?" he asks in a neutral, uninflected voice. He is wearing tinted glasses, although the day is dreary, and a .38-caliber pistol in a holster on his belt.

I nod and say yes.

"How long were you in Canada?"

As I answer eight or nine days, he scans the interior of the car.

"What were you doing there?"

I answer simply and definitively. Vacation. He pauses for an instant, his face impassive, to process this information. I can see that it doesn't sound quite right to him. Vacationing in Canada in October?

"Did you drive around the lake?" he asks.

I tell him yes.

"Traveling alone?"

I explain that my wife was with me for the first part of the trip but that I put her on a plane in Thunder Bay a few days ago. As I speak, I realize that this answer, which is a bit unusual, will only provoke more questions and scrutiny.

He stares at me silently for a minute, then glances at my passport. "What's your birthdate?" he asks casually.

I pass his first test.

"Where were you born?"

I pass his second test.

"Who do you work for?"

When I answer the federal government, and specifically the Department of the Interior, he asks me with feigned ignorance, "Oh, what do they do?"

I tell him what he already knows.

"Do you have any ID for your job?"

I hand him my federal identification badge, and he studies it for a minute.

"Will you pop the trunk for me? And stay in the car."

After he rummages briefly through the trunk, he returns to my window.

"Are you bringing back anything from Canada?"

I have made no attempt to hide anything; several plastic shopping bags lie in plain view on my back seat. Two bottles of liquor and a couple of souvenirs from the Canadian duty-free store, I tell him.

"How many bottles of liquor?" he asks.

Two, I repeat.

He shakes his head. "You're only allowed to bring back one bottle of liquor without paying duty. They'll sell you as much as you'll buy, but duty-free doesn't mean you can buy as much as you want without paying duty."

I shrug and tell him the truth: I didn't know. For a minute I think he's going to confiscate my second bottle or tell me to pull over to the parking lot on the right-hand side so that my car can be searched more thoroughly. But he already knows I'm no threat to national security, and one bottle of liquor isn't worth anyone's time. If he hassles me further, it's only because he wants to and can. In the meantime, another car has pulled up behind mine at the crossing.

"Ah, you didn't know," he says then, "so I'll let it go this time." He hands me back my passport and identification badge. "Have a nice trip," he says indifferently as he shifts his attention to the next car.

As I drive south into Michigan on Interstate 75, my immediate reaction is one of relief. As the minutes pass, however, my temper rises. I know that we live in a complicated, dangerous world (one whose current dangers, by the way, we Americans have helped create), and I know that, as a result, certain precautions are necessary, particularly at international borders. But I am a scrupulous, law-abiding person, and although a few details of my current trip may have been unusual, I question whether they justified the officious interrogation—the petty harassment—I received this morning. I am reminded of an obvious fact I often choose to ignore: that I am not immune to our government's power. By voluntarily entering (or remaining in) the United States, I am submitting myself to our government's jurisdiction. And subject to the limitations imposed on its power by the United States Constitution—the Bill of Rights, in particular—our government, acting through its officials (including low-level functionaries), may decide to question me about my activities, search my property, or intrude even further into my private life.

Which leads me to contemplate another disturbing aspect of my citizenship (and one that might help explain my reluctance to engage further with Gerald yesterday morning): that, as much as I disagree with, and would like to disavow, certain of our government's policies, I am not innocent of them. In return for accepting the benefits of American citizenship, I bear some responsibility for the conduct of the government that provides them. That is a part of the social contract. It is a thought that doesn't entirely please me, for as much as I love our country and the ideals of personal freedom and equality under the law that it espouses, I am dismayed these days by its self-righteous, crusading attitude and grandiose foreign policies. And by the price that we (and others around the world) are paying for them.

My experience at the United States' border crossing this morning probably doesn't signify anything momentous or even particularly meaningful, but I can't help thinking about my reentry into Canada yesterday afternoon, when I was returning from my visit to Mackinac Island. At the Canadian port of entry a middle-aged female Border Services Agency officer, unarmed, asked me the usual series of standard questions: What is your citizenship? What is the purpose of your visit? How long do you intend to stay in Canada? What is your destination? Do you have any firearms in your vehicle? Alcohol? Tobacco products? She then asked me how long I had been in the United States, and when I answered one day, she paused and looked at me suspiciously. I explained that I had been staying at the Glenview Vacation Cottages and had gone into the United States earlier that day to visit Mackinac Island. She looked at me again, assessing me and my story. It took her only a moment to decide that I posed no threat.

"Welcome back to Canada," she said cordially. "Glenview's a great place."

I agreed with her.

"Enjoy the rest of your stay," she said then, motioning me back into her country.

# # #

The Upper Peninsula of Michigan: The Literature of Place

> The beauty of a landscape needs help to endure in your mind. You must mentally people the landscape with human history and, more important, the sense of the quality of human life you can get only from first-rate literature. . . . A mere landscape can wear out for you like the photos of beautiful women you collected as a young man. Their power wore thin because you didn't know them, their voices, the smell and touch, the qualities of their minds.
>
> Jim Harrison, *Off to the Side: A Memoir*

The Upper Peninsula of Michigan, that part of the state lying north of the Straits of Mackinac, stretches from east to west for 350 miles along Lake Superior's southern shore. At its narrowest, near Sault Sainte Marie, the UP is barely thirty miles wide, but to the west it widens to embrace the northwestern shore of Lake Michigan, before tapering to a point near the town of Ironwood. Viewed on a map, it resembles a shark, its tail flashing in Lake Huron, its body suspended between Lakes Michigan and Superior, its head attacking northern Wisconsin. (The Keweenaw Peninsula curving northeast into Lake Superior is the shark's dorsal fin.)

For many people the UP is a fabled land of forests, rivers, lakes, and wildlife. And, I must add, of Arctic-length, snow-globe winters. In the lake-effect belt near Superior's southern shore, more than 150 inches of snow falls each winter, and in the shade of the big trees it often stays on the ground into May. Until 1957, when the Mackinac Bridge was completed, travel between lower Michigan and the UP was accomplished primarily by ferry in the summer and, for the adventuresome, by icebreaker in the winter. The bridge made the UP more accessible, but even today its population is only about three hundred thousand—about 3 percent of Michigan's population—which means that, on average, the UP is less densely populated than either Utah or Nevada.

In aboriginal times the peninsula was both revered and feared by the Ojibwe and Dakota Indians, who memorialized it in their legends and oral traditions. Their stories helped lure Euro-American trappers, miners, and lumberjacks to the area. Today, after nearly two hundred years of intensive extractive industry—primarily iron and copper mining and logging—the UP is not a pristine landscape. But because its harsh climate has defeated most attempts at settlement and cultivation, it has retained its wild character. The magnificent old-growth white pines—some of them towered more than two hundred feet high—may be gone, but a dense second- or third-growth forest of evergreen and deciduous trees—red pines, jack pines, balsam firs, hemlocks, northern white-cedars, tamaracks, maples, basswoods, beeches, aspens, and birches—still blankets the peninsula.

Today the UP, like many areas around Lake Superior, seems to be in the process of slow and sometimes painful change. The traditional extractive industries are declining, and much of the local economy now depends on the imported cash of seasonal tourists and part-time residents. The UP has long attracted "outdoorsmen" (and "outdoorswomen")—that is, people who like to hunt, fish (summer or winter), ride ATVs or snowmobiles, and generally hang out in the woods—and in recent years has served, infamously, as the home base or training ground of anti-government survivalists and gun nuts like Ted Nugent. But it is also beginning to attract a more mainstream, affluent crowd, and the timber-and-granite second homes of well-heeled urbanites are now joining the old-fashioned "tourist camps" scattered around the peninsula's inland lakes.

* * *

I am touring the UP for a few days, traveling, as is my preference, in the early fall. Driving north from Milwaukee and the city of Green Bay, I cross into Michigan over the Menominee River and follow Michigan Route 35 along the northwestern shore of Lake Michigan to Escanaba, a bustling blue-collar port and mill town near the mouth of Little Bay de Noc. Along with Marquette, located about sixty miles north on Lake Superior, Escanaba marks the western boundary of the central UP, an area that has inspired more serious literary efforts than any other around Lake Superior. I don't know why this is the case. Perhaps it is simply a function of the area's long and varied human history: oral tradition begets folklore, which begets written literature. Or perhaps it is the fact that over a long period of time people in the more populous parts of the Midwest have viewed the UP as a symbol or example of something worth writing about—a vestige of the American wilderness or a place where men and women pursue, or return to, a more elemental existence. Whatever the reason, one purpose of my trip is to visit (or revisit) this area that has loomed large in people's imaginations; to consider (or reconsider) some of the literary works it has inspired; and to spend some time pondering the connections between literature and place.

From Escanaba I drive east on US Route 2 to Manistique, where in the early evening I check into a nondescript chain motel. (After inspecting my bland accommodations, I realize, too late, that I should have stopped in Escanaba and searched out the historic House of Ludington, Jim Harrison's "favorite Midwestern hostelry.") The next morning I continue east on Route 2 and north on Michigan Route 77 to Germfask and Seney National Wildlife Refuge, arriving in time to join a guided tour of the refuge with an earnest young intern named Alice, a recent graduate of Northern Michigan University in Marquette with a degree in environmental education.

For the next couple of hours I ride shotgun as Alice drives a vanload of us (including several serious birders, a different breed altogether) on a circuit of dirt or gravel refuge roads. We skirt hummocky marshes and expansive pools of water with small wooded islands, prime habitat for bald eagles, ospreys, trumpeter swans, Canada geese, common loons, various species of ducks, and other migratory waterfowl. We wind through jack-pine forests and pine-stump fields in various states of regeneration and pass meadows where the Fish and

125

Wildlife Service scatters grain on the ground to attract birds and other animals. Alice tells us that the refuge encompasses the remnants of the Great Manistique Swamp, which was logged, burned, and drained in the early twentieth century in an unsuccessful attempt to convert it to agricultural land. After the refuge was established in 1935, the Civilian Conservation Corps constructed earthen dikes and other water control structures to impound the diffuse surface flow and create the landscape we see today.

During the tour I am surprised to learn that the refuge allows the hunting of certain upland game birds—ruffed grouse and woodcock—as well as snowshoe hare, deer, and bear. Although I have nothing against hunting or hunters, the allowance of hunting strikes me as inconsistent with the concept of a "wildlife refuge." When I ask Alice about that apparent conflict, however, she responds that one of the refuge's purposes is to provide "recreational opportunities" for "sportsmen." I tell her, somewhat contrarily, that it seems unfair, or at least unsporting, to lure wildlife to the refuge with enhanced habitat and supplemental food, and then to subject certain unlucky species to the sportsmen's fusillades. She replies that the refuge only allows the "harvest" of wildlife whose populations are "healthy." I want to tell her that that is beside the point—that it's a question of ethics, not ecology—but she doesn't seem interested in continuing this idiosyncratic conversation and the others on the van seem unconcerned about the fate of the animals we are attempting to observe, so I shut up.

The Manistique River, which meanders through the southeastern corner of the refuge en route to Lake Michigan, is the mother stream in this part of the UP. A few miles east of the refuge the Fox River contributes its flow to the Manistique. The

Fox is famous in Michigan not only as a blue-ribbon trout-fishing stream but also—particularly for men of a certain age and disposition—as the inspiration for one of Ernest Hemingway's best-known and best-loved short stories, "Big Two-Hearted River." The real Big Two-Hearted River is located nearby and, unlike the Fox, flows north into Lake Superior. Hemingway probably never saw it, but he liked its evocative name and, exercising the fiction writer's prerogative, constructed his story around it.

Hemingway visited the UP and fished the Fox with two friends in the late summer of 1919, after returning to the United States from his military service in Italy, where he had suffered a serious leg injury while driving an ambulance for the allies in World War I. Hemingway, only twenty at the time, enthusiastically described the Fox in a letter to Howell Jenkins, a war buddy and fellow fisherman: "The Fox is priceless. The big [F]ox is about 4 or five times as large as the Black [River, east of Petoskey, in lower Michigan] and has ponds 40 feet across. The little Fox is about the size of the Black and [is] lousy with them [trout]. . . . We caught about 200 and were gone a week. We were only 15 miles from Pictured Rocks on Lake Superior. Gad that is great country." Within a few years Hemingway had transformed his apparently exuberant trip to the UP with his two friends into a melancholy, solo camping and fishing trip taken by Nick Adams, his young fictional protagonist.

I should confess right here that I am not a big fan of Hemingway's prose style. I respect the man's physical prowess, his extraordinary dedication to the craft of writing, and the courageous way in which he ended his life when he believed he had exhausted his creative powers. And I recognize that he was a stylistic innovator who produced some passages of great power and beauty (including the famous opening chapter of *A Farewell to Arms*, that pointillist description of fighting on the Italian front during World War I). But over the course of a book his writing drives me nuts. So many definite and indefinite articles; so many forms of "to be"; so few adjectives and adverbs. The flat tone of narration and dialogue. The relentless ping, ping, ping of monosyllables and the insistent repetition, over and over, of words and phrases. Reading a Hemingway novel is, for me, like being subjected to Chinese water torture.

But what wears on me over the course of a novel—Hemingway's concentrated, repetitive style—is exactly what makes his short stories so powerful, and "BTHR" is one of his best. Indeed, I think it is a masterpiece of the genre. The story itself is simple and uneventful. Nick Adams arrives by train at the abandoned, burned-over town of Seney in the UP, from which he begins hiking north, following the Big Two-Hearted River toward Lake Superior. He finds a campsite near the river in the late afternoon, pitches his tent, and cooks his dinner. As he makes coffee after dinner, he briefly recalls a previous fishing trip with friends on the Black River. The next morning, after breakfast, he collects a bottle of grasshoppers and uses them as bait to catch several trout in the river. As he fishes, he moves downstream, approaching a dark cedar swamp where the water deepens and the trees grow together overhead to block the sun. The prospect of the swamp unaccountably causes him to feel a sense of fear or dread. There, "in the fast deep water, in the half-light," he thinks, "the fishing would be tragic. In the swamp fishing was a tragic adventure." He decides that he doesn't have the heart to fish the swamp that day.

Hemingway relates this simple story in minute, almost excruciating detail, from the way Nick makes his coffee after dinner to the way he baits his hooks with the grasshoppers the next morning; and that accumulating detail, combined with the flat tone and repetitive cadence of Hemingway's prose, gradually generates an ominous air. One begins to sense that Nick is trying, through his almost obsessive attention to the mundane details of camping and fishing, to control an unspoken fear or suppress a mindless frenzy, to impose order on his life.

> Nick was happy as he crawled inside the tent. He had not been unhappy all day. This was different though. Now things were done. There had been this to do. Now it was done. It had been a hard trip. He was very tired. That was done. He had made his camp. He was settled. Nothing could touch him. It was a good place to camp. He was there, in the good place. He was in his home where he had made it. Now he was hungry.

From other Nick Adams stories Hemingway's readers know that Nick is struggling to recover from the horrors of World War I—in Hemingway's now-famous phrase from *A Farewell to Arms*, Nick is searching for "a separate peace"—but the war is not mentioned in "BTHR."

Literary theorist and critic Kenneth Burke once observed, "Form in literature is an arousing and fulfillment of desires"—an elegant, incisive formulation. As readers we like conflict followed by resolution, tension followed by release. We like to have our curiosity piqued and then satisfied. In "BTHR" Hemingway violates that principle and gets away with it. In fact,

I believe that precisely what makes "BTHR" powerful is its elliptical nature—what happens between the words and lines; what, for the reader, remains unstated and unknown. We simply never learn what has happened since the last time Nick fished these northern waters.

All we get are a few—a very few—poignant clues. After dinner at his campsite, as Nick recalls his previous fishing trip on the Black River, he recollects a good-natured argument about the proper way to make coffee with one of his friends, a man named Hopkins, "the most serious man Nick had ever known." Nick and Hopkins had argued about everything. On that trip Hopkins learned, via telegram, that he had made "millions of dollars" from an oil well in Texas; he then gave his prized possessions to his companions and departed early. Before he left, however, the friends discussed next year's trip.

> They were all going fishing again next summer. The Hop Head was rich. He would get a yacht and they would all cruise along the north shore of Lake Superior. He was excited but serious. They said good-by and all felt bad. It broke up the trip. They never saw Hopkins again. That was a long time ago on the Black River.

Yes, that was a long time ago on the Black River, when the world was younger and Nick was younger, and he and his friends looked forward innocently to a future that never happened. They never saw Hopkins again.

* * *

From the wildlife refuge I continue north on Michigan Route 77, driving through the town of Seney and toward Grand Marais. For long stretches the highway runs straight and flat through an area covered with a dense second- or third-growth forest of mixed evergreen and deciduous trees that occasionally open onto wetlands where scraggly black spruces and tamaracks sprout from thickets of tag alder and willow. Unmarked driveways or logging roads appear suddenly along the highway and, when I look down them, curve and disappear just as suddenly into the dark, encroaching forest.

Traversing the UP today, one is struck by how empty and unpopulated it is. Towns are few and far between, and many that appear on the map are in reality no more than a handful of modest houses; a small, struggling business strip (often consisting only of a gas station, an IGA, and, perhaps, a Family Dollar or NAPA auto parts store); an abandoned, disintegrating motor court; and, on the outskirts of town, a hair-styling or tanning salon occupying the living room of someone's house. Older-model American-made sedans and pickup trucks with rust-eaten fenders sit forlornly at the ends of dirt driveways with hand-lettered signs taped to their windshields: "For Sale / $2800 OBO" or "Runs good / Make offer." There is little agriculture in the UP, and the derelict farmhouses and overgrown orchards along the highways are melancholy reminders of a time in the late nineteenth and early twentieth centuries when promoters marketed the land to naïve, hopeful immigrants unaware of the peninsula's long, brutal winters. ("On this back road the land / has the juice taken out of it," Jim Harrison wrote in a poem about northern Michigan, "stump fences surround nothing / worth tearing down / by a deserted filling station / a Veedol sign, the rusted hulk / of a Frazer, 'live bait' / on battered tin.")

The radio is dominated by country music, oldies rock, and syndicated talk-radio, the last, of course, consisting largely of pop psychologists dispensing tough love to their confused callers or political pundits of various stripes railing about the hot-button issues of the day. But what I have just said is, of course, a gross generalization, for in recent years radio translators have brought more diverse programming to many rural areas, including the UP, so that even here, in this remote hinterland, one can now find, at the lower end of the FM dial, stations playing classical or jazz music.

The food typically served in restaurants in the UP is not the kind that cardiologists recommend for their patients. The most popular dinner offerings are pasties, fried fish, steaks, hamburgers, and pizza. High-calorie, high-fat food to get the people through the long winters. As is true in many rural, working-class areas, cigarette smoking is still relatively common among the UP's residents, so that entering a road house along the highway one is often greeted by the unappetizing smells of cooking grease, stale cigarette smoke, and spilled beer. The UP is not, and will probably never be, a gourmet's destination.

But, of course, citified diversions and fine dining are not what draw people to the UP. Rather, what draws people here today is what has always drawn people here: vast untracked forests abounding with wildlife; myriad lakes and free-flowing rivers teeming with fish; extreme, dramatic weather; the mysterious allure of the wilderness, the big woods.

* * *

After buying some groceries in the town of Grand Marais, I turn west onto Sable Lake Road, Alger County Route H58, and wend my way into Pictured Rocks National Lakeshore, which stretches along the southern shore of Lake Superior from here to the town of Munising, about forty miles away. The road is paved for only a short distance before narrowing to a sandy, often-washboarded route that dips and curves through a dark, lovely forest en route to the Twelvemile Beach campground, located between Au Sable Point and the Pictured Rocks themselves, where I am lucky to claim the last available campsite on the lakeside of the campground loop.

Shortly after I arrive, a brief shower dampens the campground and forest, and I sit in the car and doze until it passes. As the sky clears, I rouse, climb out of the car, stretch for a few minutes, and wander down to the lakeshore, at the base of a sandy bluff behind the campsite. To the north the view from the narrow beach is clean and pacific. Beneath the pale, rain-washed sky the lake's smooth, lapis-colored surface extends beyond the earth's curve, forming a featureless horizon. The beach itself is deserted but for a man and woman a couple of hundred yards to the southwest silently wading in the sun-dappled shallows. The air is still, and the only sounds are the gentle, rhythmic soughing of the surf on the sand and a seagull's occasional caw. A benign afternoon at Twelvemile Beach.

Returning to my campsite, I open a bottle of beer that I sip as I patrol my tiny domain, examining the varied plants growing in the sandy soil (including several species of fern whose fronds have been burned by an early frost) and picking up small pieces of litter inadvertently dropped by previous campers. Then I set up my tent, unroll and inflate my Therm-a-Rest pad inside, and lay my sleeping bag on top, shaking it to fluff the down. My sleeping chamber prepared for the night, I settle at the picnic table, where I heat a simple stew on my camp stove as the late-afternoon sun fills the forest understory with oblique, liquid light. The air is balmy and aromatic, smelling faintly of pine resin and balsam, and I surrender to the peaceful mood of the day. Butterflies levitate silently in the shafts of light, and a few flies and yellow jackets, attracted by the smell of my dinner, buzz my head and table, but I am too tired or relaxed to rise to their challenge, instead gently shooing them away. Although the campground is nearly full, it is remarkably quiet, and from my picnic table I hear the wavelets lapping at the lakeshore. As I slowly eat my meal and then clean my dishes, the world begins to dissolve into dusk and darkness. Across the big lake to the north, toward Canada, a violet mist floats above the water's surface, conjuring mythic islands and worlds: Atlantis, Arcadia, Avalon.

This area is famous as the setting for Henry Wadsworth Longfellow's 1855 epic poem *The Song of Hiawatha*, which interpreted and dramatized certain Ojibwe Indian oral traditions. Longfellow, a professor at Harvard University, never visited the UP, and his *Hiawatha* is a hybrid creation of his imagination. He modeled the form of his poem on the *Kalevala*, the mythic tale often regarded as the Finnish national epic, and borrowed much of its substance from the ethnographic writings of Henry R. Schoolcraft, a prominent white American who served as the Indian agent for the Ojibwe and Ottawa tribes at Sault Sainte Marie from 1822 to 1841. Schoolcraft had become acquainted with the region in 1820, when he had been the geologist on an expedition to explore and map the Upper Great Lakes under the direction of Lewis Cass, then governor and superintendent of Indian affairs for Michigan Territory. Schoolcraft recounted his impressions of the expedition in a book dauntingly titled *Narrative Journal of Travels through the Northwestern Regions of the United States, extending from Detroit through the Great Chain of American Lakes to the Sources of the Mississippi River, Performed as a Member of the Expedition under Governor Cass, in the Year 1820.* During his tenure as Indian agent Schoolcraft married a granddaughter of an Ojibwe chief, often visited the local Indian villages, and recorded Indian culture, traditions, and lore in more than twenty scholarly and popular books.

Longfellow's poem, as many schoolchildren know even today, tells the life story, in twenty-two cantos, of an Ojibwe man-hero named Hiawatha. Born of Wenonah, the granddaughter of the moon, and Mudjekeewis, the arrogant, temperamental West Wind, Hiawatha is raised by Nokomis, his maternal grandmother, after Wenonah dies of heartbreak, when Mudjekeewis abandons her. Under Nokomis's tutelage Hiawatha learns the traditions of his people and the ways of the forest and, true to the heroic tradition, endures as he grows into manhood a series of trials, from meeting, confronting, and reconciling with his father; to wrestling with Mondamin, an emissary of the "Master of Life," whose defeated body is transfigured into maize; to battling Nahma, the armored sturgeon, in the depths of Gitche Gumee; to slaying Megissogwon, the evil Magician. Hiawatha prays and fasts, not for personal gain or aggrandizement, but for the betterment of the Indian peoples and nations. Eventually he woos and marries the beautiful Dakota maiden Minnehaha, "Laughing Water," which brings about a sort of Periclean era of peace and prosperity among the tribes. But of course that era ends, as it must, when malevolent spirits cause a series of misfortunes, culminating in a winter famine that kills Minnehaha. As is often the case—curiously—in Indian legends, Hiawatha then relates a vision of the coming of the white man to the New World and the eventual defeat of the Indian nations. Finally, in the last canto, as Hiawatha stands on the lakeshore on a bright summer morning, he is visited by "the Black-Robe chief, the Pale-face / With the cross upon his bosom." Hiawatha welcomes the priest and his entourage; invites them into his wigwam; listens politely (if noncommittally) to their Christian proselytizing; and, as his guests slumber through the hot, still afternoon, quietly departs in his canoe toward the northwest, "To the Islands of the Blessed / . . . To the land of the Hereafter!"

Hiawatha was wildly popular in its own day, selling five thousand copies in the first five weeks after publication, and remains a part, at least in edited form, of many elementary or junior high school curricula. But it was not an unequivocal success. Some contemporary critics accused Longfellow of adapting more than just the form of the *Kalevala*. Moreover, as modern literary scholar and critic Daniel Aaron observed, "[I]n borrowing *Kalevala*'s thumping, eight-syllabled trochaic verse form as the one best suited to his purpose, he left himself open to parodists unable to resist the fun of burlesquing *Hiawatha*'s tom-tom rhythms, its parallelisms and repetitions, and its plethora of what to the humorists were comical sounding Indian names." It is particularly hard for a modern reader, steeped in the facile satire of television and other popular media, to read even the first verse of *Hiawatha* without imagining sophomoric parodic riffs:

> Should you ask me, whence these stories?
> Whence these legends and traditions,
> With the odours of the forest,

With the dew and damp of meadows,
With the curling smoke of wigwams,
With the rushing of great rivers,
With their frequent repetitions,
And their wild reverberations,
As of thunder in the mountains?

Part of the problem lies in the natural evolution of language and literary taste and the passage of time, which have taken American poetry ever farther from the rigid meter and perfect rhyme of Longfellow's era. And part of the problem lies in Longfellow's decision to employ curiously formal diction ("whence") and spelling that was quaint even in his own day ("odours"). I suspect that by employing such archaisms Longfellow was striving for a certain grand effect: he was trying to write an old-fashioned epic. Unfortunately, the form and rhetorical devices he employed, tired even in his own day, have long passed out of fashion and show no sign of popular revival.

For modern readers the poem's narrative line is also problematic. *Hiawatha* is a traditional hero-tale, relating the story of a young man who ventures alone into the dangerous unknown; stoically endures hardship and privation; encounters and either defeats or befriends various supernatural beings; gains strength and knowledge through his adventures; and finally returns home to share his experiences and wisdom with his people. But many modern readers find his story uninteresting, even tedious, because Hiawatha appears to have no faults. He acts and speaks in a manner that is invariably, monotonously noble and altruistic. And when misfortune finally strikes him and his people, it is not because of an inherent tragic flaw or mistake, but because of events completely out of his control.

Which may be symbolic of the tragedy of the New World, but which is not engaging to the modern sensibility. In literature, as in life, we find fallible men more interesting than infallible gods.

* * *

The next morning I awake to a freshening breeze off the lake. The temperature is still mild, but the wind has churned the lake's surface into two- to three-foot swells that break over a sandbar a hundred yards offshore before re-forming and surging toward the beach. I decide to take advantage of the continuing warm weather to fulfill an idiosyncratic lifelong dream: to swim in Lake Superior. Surprisingly, the water temperature on this early-fall day, in the shallows at least, nearly matches the air temperature—in the low sixties. I wade carefully through the swells and finally, standing waist-deep, take the dive into deeper water. I emerge with a howl, shivering and shaking like a wet dog. But the sun, filtered by a few high cirrus clouds, provides just enough warmth to blunt the chill, and I spend fifteen or twenty minutes relishing this new experience, swimming a few strokes back and forth parallel to the beach, trying to bodysurf the larger waves, and peering at the sandy or pebbled bottom through the water's clear, refractive lens.

After a leisurely breakfast I pack up my camp and drive slowly southwest on County Route H58 to the Chapel Basin area of the national lakeshore, where I hike a 9.6-mile loop through the forest to the lake, around Grand Portal Point, and then back to the trailhead along a series of gullies and streams. For almost half its distance the trail follows the lakeshore above the Pictured Rocks themselves, strata of light-colored Cambrian sandstone forming vertical cliffs that rise as high as two hundred feet above the water and that have been stained and streaked in variegated tones of white, black, brown, red, pink, yellow, and green by manganese, iron, copper, and limonite leaching out of the rock. Thus the name, first applied by Schoolcraft during the 1820 Cass expedition, although the area was well known to the Ojibwes and was a prominent landmark for early European explorers.

In places the lake's wave action has carved alcoves and shallow caves in the base of the cliffs; sculpted the sandstone into pillars, turrets, and other fanciful shapes; and eroded ledges that overhang the lake, so that one can walk to land's end and look straight down, through the pellucid water, to the bouldery bottom twenty or thirty feet below the surface. The colors of the water on this sunny day are astonishing: from turquoise—a color I want to call "Caribbean"—at the base of the cliffs; to sapphire in the shallower water; to cobalt in the deeper; and finally to indigo far out on the lake. In several places the wind has eroded the sandstone just below the cliffs into hoodoos and other weird aeolian features that recall the arid badlands of the American West. With the pale blue northern sky arching overhead and the deep green forest stretching inland from the clifftops, the landscape is lovely—indeed, on a day like this one, almost sublime.

* * *

After completing the trail loop, I drive into Munising, where, after making some discreet inquiries at a local visitor center, I head for the Sunset Motel on the Bay, a mom-and-pop establishment located on a side street on the eastern side of town whose rooms face the water. When I enter the tidy front office, I discover that in this case mom is Carmon Decet, a blond-haired woman in her late thirties with a broad, pretty face, taut Scandinavian skin, and wolf-grey eyes. She smiles easily when I walk in, and, as is only occasionally the case in our tense, frenetic modern world, I immediately feel relaxed and comfortable around her. Although I am normally quite guarded around people I have just met, when she tells me that she rented her last room a few minutes ago, I throw up my arms and wail theatrically.

She laughs and then volunteers that she and her husband own two houses near the motel and that she will rent me one up the street with three bedrooms, a bathroom, and a full kitchen for the remarkable sum of $75 a night.

"Feel free to use the washer and dryer," she adds helpfully.

I am aware that after my time in the woods I look a bit disheveled and probably smell equivalently. (I think this is not what Longfellow meant by "the odours of the forest.")

I promptly accept her offer. In doing so, I tell her, with exaggerated seriousness, that having access to a washer and dryer means that I won't have to wear the same dirty underwear tomorrow.

Without missing a beat she smiles and responds in kind. "Well, I'm glad. My twelve-year-old son thinks it's pretty neat to do that, but most of us don't."

She wraps her mouth around each vowel and speaks in the slightly sing-song cadence typical of the UP, a legacy of the many Scandinavian immigrants who settled in the area. She looks straight at me as she speaks, her eyes wide and playful. Her blonde hair touches her shoulders.

After I register, we chat for a few more minutes, during which I learn that she and her husband, Tony, are native

"Yoopers" and that although they have visited Orlando, Phoenix, and Las Vegas—golden cities of the Sun Belt—they have no intention of leaving the UP. Carmon manages the motel, while Tony works for wages in town. In addition to their son, David, they have an eight-year-old daughter named Karlee, who rides her bike back and forth across the motel's parking lot as we talk, and a terrier named Maddie, who keeps Carmon company at the front desk and sticks her nose under the doggie-barricade to beg scratches from me.

Carmon has an unassuming air typical of rural, Midwestern women; a sort of wholesome sensuality; and a quiet competence that, I assume, comes from raising a family and managing a small business at the same time.

When I ask Carmon for a restaurant recommendation, she bites her lower lip pensively, cocks her head, and looks out the window toward the bay. At that moment she is an image of unstudied loveliness.

Later, after showering and changing clothes, I follow Carmon's recommendation, driving to a local restaurant near downtown Munising for an early dinner. There, as I devour a cheeseburger and fries, I reflect on my day: my invigorating, early-morning swim; my solitary, sweaty trek through the forest; my innocent flirtation with Carmon. This, I find myself thinking, was a Jim Harrison kind of day. A day of both physical and spiritual pursuits and pleasures.

Jim Harrison is the contemporary writer most closely associated with this area, and arguably one of the half-dozen greatest living American writers. Born in 1937, Harrison spent his boyhood in Reed City, a small town in rural lower Michigan, among his extended family, occasionally helping with chores at his grandparents' farm and hunting and fishing—sometimes alone, sometimes with his father or paternal uncles—in the woods near a family cabin outside of town. In his 2002 memoir, *Off to the Side*, he recalls a boyhood that, for all the hardships of rural life during the Depression and World War II, was nearly idyllic:

> What have I forgotten? Waking to the animal sounds that seem to comfort one, easing the soul into consciousness. There were no alarm clocks in the house. This ancient cycle was so embedded that no reminders were needed. The body's clock sufficed and through the screen window and the skein of a mosquito or fly's whine and buzz there was a sow's untroubled grunt, the muffled squeal of a piglet, the neighbor's dog, the milk truck two miles away, a cow lowing, a horse stomping a sleepy foot, and the long-awaited rooster's crow which, though it might still be dark, dispelled the inevitable night demons.
>
> What else have I forgotten? My young aunt bathing in a tin tub in the kitchen. . . .

Nothing in Harrison's early life suggested a literary calling, but as a boy he began to read voraciously, and while still a teenager he decided that he wanted to be a writer. Except for his passion for literature, he was an apathetic student, and at nineteen he left school and home, hitchhiking to New York City with ninety dollars in his pocket and a cardboard box packed with clothes, books, and a used typewriter, intent on living the bohemian life. (Harrison arrived in Greenwich Village about five years before another errant Midwesterner, Robert

Zimmerman.) Thus began a pattern of traveling between Michigan, where he intermittently pursued his academic career, and the cultural meccas on the East and West Coasts—Boston and San Francisco in addition to New York—where he pursued the literary life. Despite the cities' allure, however, he always returned home to Michigan, to his family and the rural landscapes of his youth.

Two chance, tragic events helped shape Harrison's personality and psyche. When he was seven, a careless playmate hit him with a broken bottle, blinding him in his left eye, and when he was twenty-four, a drunk driver crashed head-on into his family's car, instantly killing his father and younger sister. (At the time of the accident they were driving north from the family's home in Michigan to hunt deer on a relative's land. Harrison himself had considered joining them but at the last minute had decided not to.) The first set him apart from other children and at an early age turned his vision inward; and the second caused him to consider the larger themes that dominate his later work: life and death, flesh and spirit, the sacred and the profane. In large part, I think, his life and work since then have been attempts to resolve those essential human dualities, to accept that one cannot exist without the other—that life on earth is an indissoluble whole—and in so doing to salve his sense of loss. For solace and inspiration he has always returned to the natural world. "In the woods," he wrote in a 1991 essay, "it is still 1945, and there is the same rain on the roof that soothed my burning eye, the same wind blowing across freshwater. The presence of the coyotes, loons, bear, deer, bobcats, crows, ravens, heron and other birds that helped heal me then, are still with me now."

Harrison's literary output has been prolific. Since 1965 he has written eleven books of poetry, nine novels, four collections of novellas (many modern critics consider him one of the few masters of this difficult form), two collections of nonfiction, a memoir, and many screenplays. It wasn't until the late 1970s, however, with the publication of *Legends of the Fall* and the sale of the movie rights for the title novella that he achieved any sort of financial success. Because he is from Michigan and early in his career wrote about traditionally masculine activities—hunting and fishing, the outdoors, drinking—reviewers often likened him to Hemingway. But Harrison's male protagonists were not stalwart, stoic heroes like Frederic Henry or Robert Jordan; rather, they tended to be flawed, insecure, sometimes comically neurotic human beings. And Harrison's prose, unlike Hemingway's, was, from the beginning, profuse and exuberant. Harrison himself eschewed the comparison, often mentioning William Faulkner as an important formative literary influence, and with the publication of *Dalva* in 1988—a plains-family saga told in large part from his female protagonist's point of view—he seems to have laid the comparison to rest.

I have always thought that a more apt comparison is to Saul Bellow. In his range of tone (sometimes from tragic to comic in a single paragraph) and his ability to blend earthly matters and spiritual concerns, Harrison seems to me a rustic Bellovian. By putting it that way, I do not intend to denigrate Harrison. On the contrary, Bellow was a great writer—he won the Pulitzer Prize, three National Book Awards, and the Nobel Prize for Literature—and I think Harrison deserves to sit in his company. But Harrison's natural milieu is the country, and

Bellow was, to borrow Alfred Kazin's phrase, a walker in the city.

Physically, Harrison is a large, bearlike man—almost, it seems, a creature of the woods where he grew up. He is a man of legendary appetites and excesses—particularly gastronomic and alcoholic—and a gourmet who prepares fresh game and fish in a manner that recalls the *haute cuisine* served in the most adventuresome five-star restaurants. His prose is likewise wild and rich:

> Gullies, hummocks in swamps, swales in the middle of large fields, the small alluvial fan created by feeder creeks, undercut riverbanks, miniature springs, dense thickets on the tops of hills: like Bachelard's attics, seashells, drawers, cellars, these places are a balm to me. Magic (as opposed to the hocus-pocus of miracles) is equated to the quality of attentiveness. Perhaps magic *is* the quality of attentiveness, the ultimate attentiveness. D. H. Lawrence said that the only aristocracy is that of consciousness. Once I sat still so long I was lucky enough to have a warbler sit on my elbow. Certain of the dead also made brief visits.

And sometimes more than a little amusing, particularly when he is describing the epic road trips for which he has become well known:

> When I'm settled into my motel in the early evening, I invariably call the local radio station

for a hot dinner tip. I figure disc jockeys are layabouts like writers and they would likely know the best places to eat. This works pretty well if you're willing to settle for a little less and can develop the uncritical state of mind that is required if you're ever going to get out of bed in the first place. In Alliance, Nebraska, I had a fabulous two-pound rib steak, watched a soft-core porn film on TV, and went to an American Legion country dance, where I jumped around like a plump kangaroo to work off the protein rush.

But all is not lightness. Like many creative people, he is prone to periods of depression—seven "whoppers" in his life, by his count—and even occasional hallucinatory episodes:

> Every year or so in the late evening, usually right after I go to bed, my mind will enter a whirling fugal state where all the stops are pulled with my mind rushing all over the earth and well into space, to the depths of the ocean where the process slows and you can walk along the ocean's bottom. You're literally out of control though not at all violently, passing through the homes of friends, huts and kraals in Africa, the bottom of the Amazon's many rivers, inside the mouth of a lion, the short nap (a split second) in the heart of a whale.

The Upper Peninsula of Michigan

Geographically, Harrison's stories often originate in Michigan and then spiral outward, sometimes to the ends of the earth. That is true of four of his early novels—*Wolf*, *Farmer*, *Warlock*, and *Sundog*—and many of the essays collected in *Just before Dark*. With *Dalva* and its sequel, *The Road Home*, his focus shifted west to Nebraska. He returned to Michigan, however, with the novel *True North*, published in 2004, and its sequel, *Returning to Earth*, published in 2007. Although the two novels differ in form, together they relate the modern history of the Burketts, a prominent Marquette, Michigan, family that acquired its wealth through the ruthless exploitation of the UP's mineral and timber resources (and its people) in the nineteenth century.

True North is essentially the coming-of-age story of the family's male scion, David Burkett. In reaction to his father, the dissolute (and alcoholic) heir to the family fortune, David decides to research his family's role in the plunder of the UP's virginal resources and to atone for his family's historical misdeeds by publishing the results of his research. His project consumes him, and over the course of several years he writes hundreds of pages, finally publishing a condensed version in a dozen UP newspapers, to little notice or effect. His salvation comes only with his father's sudden, grisly death in the Gulf of Mexico, the long-deferred consequence of an unpardonable act—the rape of a friend's daughter—he had committed years before.

Returning to Earth picks up the family's story ten years later and describes the excruciating death of David's brother-in-law, Donald, from amyotrophic lateral sclerosis—Lou Gehrig's disease—and the effect of his death on those around him. Donald, the son of the Burketts' former yardman, is a simple, good-hearted man of mixed Finnish-Ojibwe blood (a combination not uncommon in the UP). He and David's sister, Cynthia, married when they were teenagers, as her family was in the throes of disintegration. Donald seems an embodiment of the UP's collective spirit, a hard-working man familiar with Ojibwe traditions who also moves quietly through the modern, non-Indian world. He wishes to be buried in Canada, north of Sault Sainte Marie, near the place where he once spent three days fasting alone in the woods, and in large part the novel is the story of how his loved ones accommodate his wishes, setting him properly, as he puts it, "on the ghost road."

The novel consists of four equal-length chapters, each narrated in the first person by a different character: first Donald; then Kenneth, the son of David's former wife, who helps care for Donald in his last days; then David; and finally Cynthia. Although the chapters are framed and arranged in chronological order, each follows its narrator's meandering stream of consciousness through time and space, with each character adding nuance or perspective to stories told by the others. The result is a fugue-like composition that, by the end of the book, artfully circles back to its beginning. (Thus in its form *RTE* is reminiscent of one of Faulkner's masterpieces, *The Sound and the Fury.* Given Harrison's admiration for Faulkner, the similarity is probably not coincidental.)

The novel's action ranges across the UP, from Iron Mountain in the west, where Kenneth visits his grandfather, a former miner crippled by a long-ago accident in a mine owned in part by the Burkett family; to Marquette, where the Burkett family's grand ancestral home overlooks the town and harbor; to Grand Marais, where David owns a ramshackle hunting cabin in the woods near the shore of Lake Superior; to the Bay Mills

Indian Community, where Donald and Cynthia raised their two children; to Sault Sainte Marie in the east, where the family crosses into Canada on Donald's last journey on earth. As is common in Harrison's novels, animals figure prominently in the story. During his three-day fast Donald is visited by various animals curious about this odd, quiet creature in their midst. A female bear and three large ravens seem to hold special significance for him, to be his personal guardians or totems. As he talks to the ravens, explaining why he is there, Donald begins to imagine the world from their perspective. That leads to a revelation, which Donald summarizes with disarming simplicity:

> In my three days I was able to see how creatures including insects looked at me rather than just how I saw them. I became the garter snake that tested the air beside my left knee and the two chickadees that landed on my head. I was lucky enough to have my body fly over the countries of earth and also to walk the bottom of the oceans, which I'd always been curious about. I was scared at one point when I descended into the earth and when I came up I was no longer there.
>   . . . I doubt if my experience was much different than anyone else who spent three days up there. It was good to finally know that the spirit is everywhere rather than a separate thing. I've been lucky to spend a life pretty close to the earth up here in the north. I learned in those days that the earth is so much more than I ever thought it was. It was a gift indeed to see all sides at once.

Returning to Earth may not be a great novel—as readers we know in the beginning what the end will be, robbing the story of dramatic tension, and the voices of Kenneth, David, and Cynthia blend together—but it is a compelling read. As always, Harrison juxtaposes mundane and ethereal matters in unexpected and provocative ways, and his prose is a force to be reckoned with. He disdains commas and unnecessary punctuation, and like a mountain torrent his sentences rush and leap from rock to cognitive rock. I read the novel straight through, swept along by the power of the language and the pleasure of discovering, in the torrent's spume and spray, new variations on Harrison's old, recurrent themes: a reverence for the natural world; a fascination with dream life; ruminations on food and cooking; spiritual meditations; and emotional and sexual longing and consummation. Or, as Harrison once put it, the whole "incalculable messiness of life."

* * *

A couple of days later, as I drive west to Au Train and then south toward Escanaba on the UP's two-laned back roads, completing my circuit, I find myself thinking about the connection between literature and place and the influence of one on the other. Physical setting is an important part of most works of literature, and what engages us as readers and draws us into a writer's world of words is often the vivid evocation of a particular time and place. Part of the craft of writing consists of selecting and describing the right sensory details to conjure that imaginary scene (the oblique sunlight on an October afternoon, a cool breeze off a rippled sapphire lake, the skittering of golden aspen leaves across dark granite). And over the course of a book those sensory details form a melodic line in what should be a rich, polyphonic work.

In an homage to James Jones, written when he died in 1977, Joan Didion observed, "Certain places seem to exist because someone has written about them. . . . A place belongs forever to whoever claims it the hardest, remembers it most obsessively, wrenches it from itself, shapes it, renders it, loves it so radically that he remakes it in his image." Didion believed that in *From Here to Eternity* Jones had accomplished that feat, had captured or created (or re-created) a particular time and place—Schofield Barracks and Honolulu on the eve of World War II, the world that Prewitt, Warden, Maggio, and the other characters in the novel so memorably inhabit.

As usual, Didion's sharp intellect and clean prose cut to the heart of the matter. A good writer can create an imaginary world that has as much cognitive and emotional weight as the one we inhabit day to day. Thus Faulkner's Yoknapatawpha County seems to me as real and substantial as any actual location in Mississippi. And if a good writer incorporates into his or her work an actual place—particularly a place we know—then the writing can alter our perception of it, so that reading his or her work is like walking outside on a bright summer day and putting on polarized sunglasses. Suddenly that place—and maybe it's a place we've lived all our lives—seems less ordinary, more vivid than it ever did before.

I think about the UP—and, indeed, about the entire Lake Superior region—and the writers who have incorporated it into their work. Has it, I wonder, yet found its definitive interpreter, its oracle, its voice? Because Hemingway remains, even sixty years after his death, an iconic, larger-than-life figure, his image looms over those of all other writers. Most of the Nick Adams stories, however, are set in northern lower Michigan, and collectively they fill only a slender volume. For the past century and a half Longfellow's *Hiawatha* has been the work most closely associated with the Lake Superior area; despite its faults (and the ravages of time and literary fashion), the poem retains a certain primal power. But no one would argue that it has preempted the field. UP native and Michigan Supreme Court justice John D. Voelker, writing under the pen name Robert Traver, featured the UP in several of his novels, including his best-selling *Anatomy of a Murder* (later made into a critically acclaimed movie starring James Stewart and Lee Remick), and in numerous essays and articles, including a beautiful paean to fly-fishing titled "Testament of a Fisherman," which is still much loved and widely reproduced. But his readership and renown are otherwise limited.

Two writers associated with the larger region deserve mention. Sigurd Olson wrote nine books of essays in which he evoked, through his flinty prose and taciturn persona, the landscape and culture of the Boundary Waters of northeastern Minnesota. But Olson was a miniaturist—for the most part he devoted himself to the careful observation and description of the glaciated spit of rock he called "Listening Point"—and rarely mentions nearby Lake Superior in his work. Aldo Leopold wrote elegant, prescient essays about conservation from his farm in southern Wisconsin but, to the best of my knowledge, never approached the big lake.

So, in the end, I return to Jim Harrison. Although he is a native of lower Michigan and not the UP, Harrison has long been drawn to this place, and it has exerted a strong influence on his life and work. He has incorporated its landscapes into his fiction, poetry, and essays, and his best work evokes its wildness, beauty, and desolation. More than any other writer, he has staked his claim, embracing it as no one else has. But is that enough? In recent years Harrison's work has gained a large audience and garnered international acclaim, and I am confident that, at least during the author's lifetime, it will continue to be read and discussed in both popular and scholarly forums. But whether it will ultimately be accorded the elevated status of literature—whether it has the requisite mass and gravity—is another question, and one I cannot answer with any certainty, because I feel too close to the work, and am wary of critical myopia.

Perhaps it is appropriate, then, that as I continue to drive toward Escanaba, I find myself thinking about the writer Harrison admires as much as any other, William Faulkner, a man universally recognized as one of the world's great writers. In the opening lines of one of his most famous novellas, in a setting far removed from the UP and Lake Superior, he captured the spirit and allure of the wilderness this area still contains and represents:

> There was a man and a dog too this time. . . .
>
> He was sixteen. For six years now he had been a man's hunter. For six years now he had heard the best of all talking. It was of the wilderness, the big woods, bigger and older than any recorded document:—of white man fatuous enough to believe he had bought any fragment of it, of Indian ruthless enough to pretend that any fragment of it had been his to convey. . . . It was of the men, not white nor black nor red but men, hunters, with the will and hardihood to endure

and the humility and the skill to survive, and the dogs and the bear and deer juxtaposed against and reliefed against it, ordered and compelled by and within the wilderness in the ancient and unremitting contest according to the ancient and unmitigable rules which voided all regrets and brooked no quarter. . . .

The places of literature endure in the mind.

# # #

The Keweenaw Peninsula, Michigan: The Sounds of Human Enterprise

The face of the country is rugged and seamed and worn. Were it not for its mineral wealth it would remain permanently a wilderness.

"The Upper Peninsula of Michigan," *Harper's New Monthly Magazine* (May 1882)

Like a finger beckoning to distant Isle Royale, the Keweenaw Peninsula curves northeast into Lake Superior for more than eighty miles from the mainland of Michigan's Upper Peninsula, tapering to a tip at Keweenaw Point. US Route 41, a rolling, two-laned road, traces a route along the peninsula's rocky spine, terminating in the tiny hamlet of Copper Harbor. Except for occasional signs of bygone industry that appear unexpectedly along the highway's verge—derelict brick smokestacks, crumbling concrete foundations, rusting iron pipes—the peninsula seems an untouched remnant of the natural world, a quiet, sparsely populated land of forests, ridges, small glacial lakes, and the dark, rocky shores of Superior itself. Beyond Houghton and Hancock, midway out the peninsula, the settlements thin into nothingness, and here, on a still day in the deep woods, separated from the rest of the world by Superior's immensity, one can almost hear, or feel, the big lake's mysterious thrum.

The landscape's present peacefulness, however, belies its turbulent past. The peninsula is underlain by copper-rich igneous and sedimentary rock, primarily basalt and conglomerate, both of which outcrop in numerous places along its length. Long before European contact American Indians came here to search for nuggets of pure copper that appeared—miraculously, it seemed—on the surface of the ground, and in 1841 Dr. Douglass Houghton, Michigan's first state geologist, confirmed the existence of large underground copper deposits in the area, thereby precipitating the first mineral rush in the United States. For the next eighty years the Keweenaw was the scene of cacophonous human activity, as mining companies financed by wealthy investors on the East Coast established a series of company towns on the peninsula and recruited to the area thousands of miners from Cornwall, Ireland, Scotland, Germany, Finland, Italy, and eastern Europe—men willing to perform back-breaking labor for a dollar a day to extract copper from formations and fissures deep beneath the earth's surface.

During their peak in the late nineteenth and early twentieth centuries the Keweenaw mines employed fifteen thousand men and accounted for a sixth of the world's copper production. Among the best-known mines were the Calumet and Hecla, near the town of Red Jacket (later renamed Calumet in the mine's honor), and the Quincy Mine, near the town of Hancock. For decades those mines generated enormous profits and wealth and stimulated the development of this isolated part of the state. Some measure of prominence followed. Around the turn of the last century, according to local folklore, Red Jacket lost a bid to be named Michigan's new capital by a single vote in the state legislature. At that time the three counties in Michigan's so-called Copper Country—Keweenaw, Houghton, and Ontonagon—had a combined population of a hundred thousand people, and the company towns bustled to the sounds of industry, commerce, and the miners' polyglot voices.

But by then the copper districts in Montana and Arizona were producing ore more cheaply by exploiting richer, shallower deposits, while the costs of extracting the Keweenaw's ever-deeper copper only increased. Although the peninsula's mines achieved record production and earned record profits during World War I, the resurgence was short-lived. The domestic copper market crashed during the 1920s, and the Great Depression further devastated the area's economy. Except for a modest revival of activity during World War II, when the federal government subsidized copper production, the Keweenaw steadily lost population, and the peninsula slowly returned to an earlier time, to the deep and abiding quietude of the natural world, the wordless quietude that underlies the transient, noisome sounds of human enterprise.

* * *

Keweenaw is an Ojibwe word meaning "the crossing place." In aboriginal times the Indians established a canoe route across the peninsula to avoid the long detour around Keweenaw Point as they paddled along Lake Superior's southern shore. The Portage Lake Ship Canal, a deep-water channel constructed after the Civil War, follows the old canoe route, slicing across the peninsula from southeast to northwest, severing the peninsula from the mainland at the finger's first knuckle. Today the cities of Houghton and Hancock face each other across the canal, a reminder of the importance of waterborne commerce in the nineteenth century. Although both originated as shipping points for the nearby copper mines, each has developed a distinctive personality. Houghton, the home of Michigan Technological University, is a small, prosperous American city, with a lively downtown of motels, shops, and restaurants catering to the college crowd and modern suburban neighborhoods climbing the hills to the south. Across the water Hancock seems, by contrast, a working-class enclave of the Old World, with thrift stores on its main street and clapboard houses stacked up the hills to the north. It is the home of Finlandia University, a small institution founded in 1896 by Finnish immigrants primarily to educate Lutheran pastors.

Occupying a prominent site on a ridge several hundred vertical feet above downtown Hancock are the sprawling surface works of the Quincy Mine. The surviving works include the hoist house, which is a large, well-preserved brick building, and the Quincy Number Two shaft house, a large, metal-sheathed structure that resembles a rectilinear grain silo. Today those structures rise in the middle of a desolated area that looks like nothing so much as ground zero of an explosive blast, surrounded by acres of concrete, brick, and wooden debris and pieces of derelict, rusted mining equipment: stanchions, cables, trams. This is what remains of the enterprise that for seventy-five years, beginning in 1846, was one of the most profitable mines on the Keweenaw. After World War I, however, its glory days quickly faded. Although the mine survived the copper-market crash of the 1920s and the Great Depression, it closed when federal subsidies for the copper-mining industry ended after World War II. Today the site is owned by the Quincy Mine Hoist Association, a nonprofit organization that preserves and interprets it as a "heritage site" within the recently established Keweenaw National Historical Park.

On a cool, cloudy August morning—my first full day on the Keweenaw—I buy a ticket and join about ten other people on one of the association's guided mine tours. The tour begins in the brick hoist house—a surprisingly ornate structure, considering its industrial function—where we meet our guide, a dark-haired, well-spoken young man named Jake. As we select hard hats and insulated jackets from a rack of well-used equipment and clothing, Jake answers a few preliminary questions and tells us, by way of introduction, that he is a geology student at Michigan Tech and that he grew up in nearby Marquette, Michigan. True to his origins, he speaks with the round-voweled, slightly sing-song accent distinctive of the Upper Peninsula. His manner is cordial, professional, and authoritative.

As we exit the hoist house, Jake directs our attention to a radio tower far across the highway to the north; at the point of our deepest penetration into the mine, he says, we will be standing approximately underneath that tower. We then board a cog railway car and ride it half a mile down the southern side of the ridge to an adit, or horizontal passage, that now provides access to the mine. Visitors usually ride a tractor-pulled wagon through the adit, but today the tractor has mechanical problems, so we walk. The adit's original purpose was to drain groundwater pumped from the mine's lower levels. Since the mine ceased production and the pumps were turned off, the water has risen steadily to this level, where it collects and flows out of the mine in a small stream on one side of the adit. As a result, our walk into the mine is damp. And chilly. As we leave the sunlight behind, the ambient air temperature quickly drops to 43°F.

The adit enters the mine at level seven. The different levels, Jake explains, were developed at about one-hundred-foot intervals along the inclined shaft; by the time the mine closed, it had reached the ninety-second level, more than nine thousand feet down the shaft. Because the shaft followed the dip of the productive geologic formation—about 55° off horizontal—the ninety-second level was more than six thousand vertical feet below the earth's surface. The temperature rose as the miners drilled and blasted ever deeper into the earth's crust; at the ninety-second level it was close to a hundred degrees Fahrenheit.

We walk slowly through the darkening adit, stepping across or around puddles of water, following Jake and his powerful flashlight. We pass a couple of trams that were used to transport ore and waste rock through the mine on a once-extensive system of tracks. We also pause to enter, through a door that appears unexpectedly in the adit's rock wall, a dank and dimly lit room—the electricity for the wan lights supplied by a waterproof cable laid along the ground—where until recent years Michigan Tech held mining-engineering classes. (The scene in the room, furnished with old-fashioned student desks and a blackboard, is surrealistic and slightly ridiculous, like a set in a Harry Potter movie.) As we emerge from the room, Jake directs our attention overhead, where, as part of their training, Michigan Tech students bolted to the adit's basaltic ceiling polygonal steel plates of various sizes and shapes; in active mines plates like these provide additional structural support in unstable passages.

Finally, almost half a mile from where we entered the adit, with the outside world now only a pinhole of light at the end of the long, dark tunnel, we intersect a perpendicular horizontal passage. This one, known as a drift, provided lateral access to the mine's various working areas and shafts. Unlike the adit, which has been enlarged to accommodate public access, the drift, Jake says, is as the miners left it and is a more constricted passage. We turn right (east?) and follow the drift a short distance to a large, irregularly shaped chamber, known as a stope, at the far end of which the Quincy Number Five shaft rises toward the surface. The stope's floor is narrow and level; its left wall is nearly vertical; and its right wall rises obliquely outward to a high, uneven ceiling. From our perspective, then, its cross-section is roughly trapezoidal. The miners, Jake tells us, created this chamber in the 1850s or 1860s as they followed the copper-bearing formation along its 55° dip, stepping deeper and deeper into the earth. This stope was one of several working areas on level seven where the miners found and removed copper-rich amygdales, or almond-shaped vesicles, from the basaltic matrix.

Leaning against the stope's nearly vertical wall are examples of two miners' drills. The first, utilized in the mine's early years, is simply an octagonal steel bit, the size of a long broom handle, with a chiseled tip. It weighs about thirty pounds.

One man's job was to hold the bit's shaft on his shoulder, its tip against the wall, and slowly rotate it deeper into the rock as two other men alternately struck the blunt end with eight-pound sledges. The second, a later innovation, is a compressed-air, one-man hammer drill mounted on a steel pedestal. Although it looks safer to me—the risks associated with the three-man operation seem significant, especially given that the miners often worked exhausting ten-hour shifts and accidents tend to happen when one is tired—Jake says that the miners resisted the one-man drill because it disrupted long-established work teams, often consisting of family members, and because it was, either in fact or in the miners' eyes, less safe. (Other miners, working farther away, might not be aware of an accident or respond as quickly.) The companies' decision to force the miners to use the more cost-effective one-man drill was an important factor precipitating the 1913 strike at the Keweenaw mines, an event that shadows the peninsula to this day.

The miners drilled the holes into the rock walls for the placement of explosive shots—first black powder, then nitroglycerine oil, later dynamite. Jake explains that the miners drilled during the week so that the explosives could be detonated on Saturday morning, which allowed two days for the noxious fumes to dissipate and the suffocating dust to settle before the miners reentered the mine on Monday morning. As the miners began the process of drilling new holes, other underground workers, known as trammers, moved or "mucked" the blasted rock to trams located on the system of tracks, loaded the rock, and pushed the trams to nearby shafts. There they dumped the rock into wheeled containers, known as skips, that were hoisted up the tracked shafts and out of the mine. (Tramming, Jake tells us, was brutish work: the tracks often were rough and uneven, and loaded trams weighed as much as eight thousand pounds. Moreover, the work was extraordinarily dangerous: passing back and forth through recently blasted drifts and stopes, trammers were constantly exposed to the threat of rockfall.) Meanwhile, other workers resumed construction of massive timber bulwarks to support unstable walls and ceilings.

As Jake describes the mine's operation, I slowly begin to comprehend and appreciate what he is saying: that the miners created the entire chamber in which we are standing by drilling and blasting solid basalt. I am incredulous: the chamber resembles a cavernous auditorium or theater. I ask him if the basalt contained any natural cavities that the miners were able to exploit. No, Jake says again, the chamber in which we are standing is entirely man-made. ("Man-made" is technically correct; Jake also informs us that women were not allowed to work in the mine.) I walk over to the stope's vertical wall and touch the basalt; it is hard, dense rock. Contemplating the enormous labor required to create this chamber, which is but one of many such chambers on each of the mine's ninety-two levels, I suddenly feel very puny and insignificant.

With my hand still on the rock I imagine the sounds of the mine as the men worked: in early years the hard ring of steel sledges on steel bits; in later years the staccato beat of compressed-air drills; always the clastic sound of rock shattering or cleaving; and always the miners' mingled voices speaking English, Cornish, Gaelic, German, Finnish, Italian, and other languages. (Both "adit" and "stope," Jake tells us, are Cornish words.) Talking to each other as they worked or ate lunch; occasionally laughing or singing at day's end; too often shouting for help when an accident occurred, as the accidents inevitably did. (By the early twentieth century the Keweenaw mines were averaging more than one fatality per week.)

As I continue to stand with my hand on the cold basalt, my mind momentarily loosens from the moorings of ordinary reality and drifts away from the physical world as I normally experience and understand it, and I find myself wondering if, on a molecular level, the sounds of the men's voices continue to reverberate in the rock; wondering if, in some fantastical way, the basalt captured and recorded the mean drama of the miners' lives; wondering if, standing here now, I can feel those vibrations and in a sense hear those voices through my fingertips on the rock.

Jake describes for us the evolution of the miners' lighting—from tallow and stearine candles to paraffin and carbide lamps to powerful electrical lights—and asks us if we would like to experience the mine's "natural light." Of course we say yes. He extinguishes his flashlight, and we stand for a few minutes quietly in a darkness to which human eyes never adjust. It is the darkness of the earth's interior; of overcast, moonless nights; of deep, dreamless sleep. Although no one says anything, after just a couple of minutes I begin to sense nervousness in the group, and when Jake re-illuminates his flashlight, people suddenly laugh and chatter for a moment in relief.

As we relax again in the security of his light, Jake explains the reason for all this underground effort. The ore-bearing rock that was removed from the Quincy Mine was transported to a company-owned mill on nearby Torch Lake for crushing and separation and then to a company-owned smelter for purification, after which the molten copper was ladled into molds to produce ingots of various shapes and sizes. The ingots were then stockpiled on the company's dock and, during Lake Superior's ice-free months, shipped to markets in the eastern United States, where the copper was put to a myriad of uses: to sheath the wooden hulls of ships; to roof buildings; to fabricate water pipes and electrical and telephone wire; and, alloyed with zinc and tin, to produce brass and bronze for tools, weapons, and hardware.

After Jake concludes, we walk slowly back through the drift and out the adit, finally emerging into the world above ground—"going to grass," as the miners used to say—momentarily blinded by a clearing sky that seems preternaturally bright. We then ride the cog railway car back to the top of the ridge and return to the hoist house, where we surrender our hard hats and jackets and Jake delivers us into the custody of a no-nonsense young woman named Jennifer. Jennifer gives us a brief tour of the cavernous hoist house, where we inspect and admire the giant Nordberg steam-powered hoist, which, when it was installed in 1920, was the largest in the world. As the miners went deeper and deeper into the earth, more and more powerful and elaborate machines were needed to transport men and supplies to the mine's lower levels and to remove ore-bearing and waste rock from it. By 1920 the company's profit margins were shrinking, and the company constructed the ornate brick hoist house and installed the Nordberg hoist in part to impress and reassure its anxious investors toward the end of the mine's economic life. The hoist was used only until 1931, when the Quincy Mine suspended operations and laid off all but a skeleton crew. Except for a brief period of government-subsidized activity during World War II, the mine never operated again.

* * *

After completing the tour, I drive north out of Hancock on Michigan Route 203 along the Portage Lake Ship Canal and then east toward the town of Calumet. For a short distance, before it curves inland, the highway touches the shore of Lake Superior, whose surface, under the clearing sky, has acquired a rich ultramarine hue. Then, a mile and a half west of Calumet, on an elevated site with a distant view of the lake, it passes the historic Lake View Cemetery—a lovely spot, I think, for one's final rest.

As I drive, I think about the Quincy Mine, and my thoughts predictably take a melancholy turn. The miners, most of them immigrants whose names and faces are lost to us today, expended their lives here, laboring in obscurity to produce copper for a young, growing nation and, in the process, to generate wealth for sophisticated people living in faraway cities. They earned modest wages and lived simple lives, and they met different ends: some were injured or died underground, while others simply worked until they were no longer able. But in the long run their individual fates mattered little, because economic and political forces beyond their control caused the mines to close, and the miners—those who were still here—moved on, leaving behind the silent underground labyrinths, darkened and slowly filling with cold water, that today are their only lasting legacy.

From Calumet I drive northeast a short distance on US Route 41 to Ahmeek before turning left and jogging onto Five Mile Point Road, a two-laned county road that takes me back to Lake Superior's shore and along it to the town of Eagle River. Most of the route passes through dark, dense, apparently pristine forests. Despite its appearance, however, the Keweenaw is not true wilderness, and little of the land is publicly owned. Today most of the peninsula is owned by commercial timber companies, who acquired it from the mining companies as the latter were winding down their operations. The mining companies, in turn, had acquired it from the federal government in the years following the original copper discovery and rush. (The peninsula is part of a larger area that the Ojibwes ceded to the United States through the March 23, 1843, Treaty of La Pointe, after the usual questionable negotiations between the federal government and the Indians. Article V of the treaty states bluntly, "The Indians residing on the Mineral district shall be subject to removal therefrom at the pleasure of the President of the United States.") The timber companies allow some public access in return for a tax benefit under state law, but they continue to hold and manage the lands for their own corporate purposes.

The towns along the peninsula's curving northwest coast—Eagle River, Eagle Harbor, and Copper Harbor—developed at the sites of natural harbors as shipping points for the nearby copper mines. Now all are struggling to reinvent themselves as tourist destinations. And a struggle it is. In 1944 historian Grace Lee Nute, reflecting on the peninsula's hard times during the Great Depression and World War II, mused, "With peacetime driving restored, the tourist trade can be the solution to the unemployment problem." But Nute was, I fear, overly optimistic. The peninsula is remote from major metropolitan areas—the city of Houghton is 550 miles from Detroit, 400 miles from Chicago, and 350 miles from the Twin Cities—and it is not on the road to anywhere. One must want to go there, and one must make an effort to get there. The deep winter snows, though attractive to winter sports enthusiasts, make access even more difficult, and the rising price of gasoline doesn't bode well for the future tourist trade.

Nevertheless, at least during the short summer season, the peninsula can be a busy, crowded place. Especially near the paved roads that traverse it, the air seems to buzz with the sounds of motorized American tourists, like persistent, slightly annoying bees. Although many drive RVs or full-sized pickup trucks towing travel trailers, many others drive large motorcycles, mostly Harley-Davidsons. (H-D may be the preferred brand in this area because of Midwesterners' allegiance to the Milwaukee-based company.) I have always found it curious that bikers, who pride themselves on their image as outlaws or rugged individualists, often travel in large, organized groups. They form phalanxes on the road and encamp for the night like Roman legions. Sometimes they generate a lot of noise, and during the three days I spend on the peninsula, I often hear their machines' loud, guttural exhausts.

Today, after passing through Eagle River and Eagle Harbor, I take the scenic route over Brockway Mountain, arriving in Copper Harbor in the late afternoon. I had planned to camp in the area, but after inspecting the close-quartered, jam-packed campground at nearby Fort Wilkins State Historic Park (and learning that a tent site would cost me $28), I decide instead to take a room at the King Copper Motel in town. The King Copper is a throwback to an earlier era—a funky motor court, constructed during the post-World War II travel boom, where guests still park at their room's front door. Its two flat-roofed, single-story wings are arranged in a "V" embracing a small lawn that opens toward the quiet harbor, and its office occupies a separate, shoebox-sized building with a large picture window and a jaunty overhead sign that for some reason reminds me of a Nash automobile.

The King Copper was evidently renovated in the 1970s, as it features an exterior frieze of cedar shingles—a favorite motif of that architecturally impaired decade—and interior decorations that include brown shag carpet, walnut-veneer furniture, and green paisley bedspreads. The bathroom tile is shocking pink. But the King Copper is clean, comfortable, and well maintained, and after unpacking my bag, I cruise through town, looking for a likely spot for dinner. None of the restaurants strikes my fancy, however, so I return to the room, having decided to cook a simple freeze-dried dinner on the back porch. There I fire up my camp stove and, after putting on a pot of water to boil, sit in a plastic patio chair to watch the comings and goings of people around the harbor.

Shortly after I settle in, two middle-aged couples arrive on motorcycles and check into rooms across from mine in the motel's other wing. The men soon meet on one room's back porch to talk and smoke. Both are bearded and paunchy, and both are dressed in what I recognize as the Harley-Davidson rider's uniform: colorful bandannas on their heads, T-shirts under black leather vests, jeans with black leather belts and wallet chains, and black leather riding boots. They are talkative after the day's ride, and across the lawn I hear them clearly as they discuss the news headlines from Iraq and Afghanistan, the restaurant where they ate lunch, the condition of the Keweenaw's roads, and the Detroit Lions' prospects in the upcoming NFL season. They speak in loud, hearty voices (laced with the usual profanity), and I suppose I shouldn't begrudge them their camaraderie at day's end, but I am tired from my own travels, and their bravado further saps my energy. As soon as my water boils, I retire indoors to eat a quiet dinner at the walnut-veneer table in my comfortable, funky throwback room.

* * *

The town of Calumet occupies a central location along the Keweenaw Peninsula's copper-rich spine. Today the town is a husk of its former self, the impressive two- and three-story brick buildings lining its downtown streets vacant except for street-level storefronts catering to the summer tourist trade. Surrounding the town like the war-ravaged outskirts of a besieged city are the derelict surface works of the Keweenaw's most famous and profitable mine, the Calumet and Hecla. For almost a century C&H was the dominant economic and political force in this part of Michigan. At its peak the company employed five thousand men, owned almost two hundred thousand acres of land, and accounted for more than half the copper produced from the Lake Superior region. During its heyday, according to Grace Lee Nute, C&H paid a total of more than $110 million in dividends on a capital investment of only $2.5 million.

The enterprise originated in 1858, when a surveyor named Edwin Hulbert discovered a cache of pure native copper in a curious man-made pit. Hulbert initially supposed that the pit overlay a deposit of native copper that a group of Indians had worked at some point in the past, but he found no tools or other evidence to support his theory. After further investigation he concluded that the cache of native copper had not been mined locally; at the same time he realized that the pit, by sheer coincidence, overlay a lode of copper-rich conglomerate. He began acquiring land in the area and, with the assistance of some Boston investors, founded two companies, the Calumet Mining

Company and the Hecla Mining Company, to capitalize the venture. But Hulbert had difficulty bringing the mines into production, and he soon lost control of the companies to one of his prominent investors, Quincy Shaw. Shaw asked his brother-in-law, Alexander Agassiz, son of the renowned Harvard naturalist Louis Agassiz, to go to the Keweenaw to evaluate the operations. Agassiz was enthusiastic about the mines' commercial prospects and stayed on the peninsula for several years as superintendent. By 1870 the mines were operating at a profit, and a year later the two companies merged. Agassiz returned to Boston and became president, a position he held for almost forty years, until his death in 1910.

Calumet and Hecla was, as the saying goes, both lucky and good. Its conglomerate lode was extraordinarily rich—as much as 15 percent copper in the early years, compared to the 2-4 percent common in other mines in the area—and Agassiz ran the company in an efficient, autocratic manner. The results were spectacular. Larry Lankton, a contemporary Copper Country historian, summarized C&H's significance thus:

> Calumet and Hecla dominated the Lake Superior copper industry. Until the rise of Copper Range Consolidated in the early twentieth century, C&H had no legitimate rivals, and it ruled its region with a haughty self-assuredness that the only way to mine copper, or to run a mining community, was the C&H way. It became the principle [sic] magnet for immigrants. It set the standards for wages, for company paternalism, for technologies. And because Boston investors had launched C&H, after 1870 that eastern city

became the most important home of money still to be invested in the Lake Superior copper district—and of money taken out of that district in dividends. As one wag wrote in 1928: "The four greatest words in the annals of New England are Concord and Lexington and Calumet and Hecla. The first two made New England history and the last two made New England fortunes."

During Agassiz's long presidency Calumet and Hecla practiced a form of corporate paternalism originally necessitated by geographic circumstance. In the mines' early years the Keweenaw was a remote, rugged wilderness, and to recruit and retain good workers, the company needed to provide basic amenities for the men and their families: housing, stores, churches, schools, libraries, a hospital, and some forms of entertainment. (Other, illegal forms the company tolerated but did not provide.) Over time, as the mines proved their economic worth, more people migrated to the area and established nearby towns, some of which grew to substantial size, but the company continued to provide many amenities, in part because its workers had come to expect them and in part because its managers believed that providing (or withholding) them allowed the company a greater measure of control over its potentially unruly work force. The company rewarded obedient workers, for example, with subsidized company housing, while less compliant ones were left to fend for themselves in nearby communities, where housing was more expensive and less convenient. By the turn of the century C&H had constructed more than seven hundred houses on its lands, but demand still far exceeded supply, and when a vacancy occurred, the company exercised its discretion carefully.

For several decades the paternalistic system worked well, at least from the company's point of view, and the workers tolerated and accepted it. Toward the end of the nineteenth century, however, the labor movement that was sweeping through various American industries began to infiltrate the Keweenaw mines. Agassiz, the "staunch autocrat," was adamantly opposed to unionization or any other development that might impede his ability to run the company as he saw fit. In 1872 he had offered his workers a substantial raise to try to settle a strike at Calumet and Hecla; their rejection of his offer had led him to adopt subtler, more cynical methods. After the turn of the century he and James MacNaughton, the mine superintendent, carefully monitored factors that might contribute to worker unrest—wages and working conditions at other mines, for example—sometimes offering a small raise or other modest concession when they sensed the first signs of agitation. After labor organizers began to appear on the Keweenaw, they hired private detectives to monitor the organizers' activities and limited assemblies of workers on company property. They lobbied against labor reforms in the state legislature; pressured local and regional newspapers to publish stories supportive of the company; and carefully screened (i.e., censored) books and other reading material in the local, company-controlled library. And they practiced discrimination in hiring and firing to rid their work force of particular ethnic groups that they deemed troublesome.

More than any other group, Agassiz targeted the Finns. At one time all the mines in the area had recruited Finns, who had reputations as hard workers and who were not deterred by the Keweenaw's isolation and harsh climate. Early Finnish immigrants had tended to come from that country's northern, rural provinces and to be rustic, well-behaved Lutherans. By the turn of the century, however, Finnish immigrants were coming from the country's southern, more urban areas and had been politicized by Finland's struggle for independence from Czarist Russia. They had resisted Russian domination—sometimes violently—and they came to the United States with what many perceived as a socialist political bent. Moreover, although nearly all the Finns were literate in their own language, they were slow to learn English and often kept their own company, and mine managers came to regard them as clannish and insular. Most of the Finns who came to the United States had no mining experience, and they tended to work in unskilled, low-paying positions, often as underground trammers. The introduction of the one-man drill, which eliminated many miners' positions, effectively eliminated their chances for advancement to better-paying jobs. Thus the Finns were particularly receptive to the labor organizers' persuasion and promises.

Although Agassiz and other mine owners and managers effectively foiled labor organization for many years, after 1910 representatives of the Western Federation of Miners finally gained a foothold on the Keweenaw. Founded in Butte, Montana, in 1893, the WFM was, by all accounts, a radical organization. It openly (and proudly) espoused socialist doctrines, and the preamble to its constitution boldly declared that a class struggle existed within society, that workers were being exploited, and that the class struggle would continue "until the producer is recognized as the sole master of his product." The union also often used inflammatory rhetoric to incite its members to violence. The WFM's tactics had produced bloodshed and murder in the mining districts of Cripple Creek, Colorado, and Coeur d'Alene, Idaho. Before his death in 1910 Agassiz had vowed never to negotiate with the union. As the Keweenaw copper companies began to mandate use of the one-man drill, however, local membership in the WFM increased dramatically. By 1913 the union claimed nine thousand members out of a total work force of fifteen thousand. In early July of that year the local union demanded a conference with employers "to adjust wages, hours, and working conditions in the copper district of Michigan." If the employers refused, then the union was prepared to order a strike. The long era of peaceful corporate paternalism on the Keweenaw was about to end.

* * *

As I was driving to Copper Harbor yesterday, I paused in Eagle Harbor and discovered the Lake Breeze, a small inn located directly on the basaltic shore of Lake Superior. The inn occupies a post-and-beam building constructed in 1859 by a Quaker merchant, William P. Raley, as a warehouse to supply the nearby mines. In the 1920s his son and daughter-in-law converted the property to a small summer resort. Today the inn is operated by Marcia Raley, William P.'s great-granddaughter, and her partner, Chris Kvale. Marcia is a tall, slender woman with graying, shoulder-length hair, bifocal glasses, and a crisp but friendly manner. She and Chris live in Minneapolis but return to the Keweenaw each year to operate the inn from late June through late August. Marcia didn't have any vacancies for last night, but after inspecting the tidy premises—downstairs the well-kept, book-filled common room and upstairs the small, quaint guest rooms, each with knotty-pine paneling, birchbark

175

picture frames, and handmade quilts on the beds—I made a reservation for tonight.

I arrive back in Eagle Harbor, however, a couple of hours before I can check in. As I pull onto the highway's shoulder to consider what to do in the meantime, I notice a small sign pointing the way to the local cemetery. Because cemeteries can be interesting, even pleasant places to pass the time, I turn and drive through a modest neighborhood to the outskirts of town. The Pine Grove Cemetery, as its name suggests, is located in a stand of stately red and white pines on a ferny hillock surrounded by a denser, darker forest. I turn off the car's engine and step outside into a peaceful natural scene. The air smells faintly of pine resin and dry duff, and the only sounds are the trilling of a few small birds and the occasional soughing of a light wind in the high branches: blessed quiet. The history of a place is often written in shorthand in the local cemetery. The Pine Grove Cemetery is attractively unkempt (as a country graveyard should be) and appears to be as old as the town itself, so I spend the next couple of hours walking up and down its sandy, needle-cushioned lanes, reading the various markers and contemplating the history of this part of the Keweenaw.

Several of the older headstones memorialize young Cornishmen who died in the mines. A simple, worn one marks the final resting place of a man named Dunstone—no first name—born in Camborne, Cornwall, who died on January 10, 1868, at age twenty-four. Nothing more. Another, erected for Mathew Wasley, a native of Cox Hill, Cornwall, who died in 1873 at age twenty-two, bears a cautionary epitaph of the kind popular in the Victorian era: "Reader, one moment stop and think, for thou art on the eternal brink." A few headstones are inscribed in German. The Finns, separate even in death, occupy their own section in the southeastern corner of the cemetery, with headstones for Tuoriniemi, Leskinen, and Haataja and family plots for Pellikka and Kumpula. Although infant and child mortality was high in the nineteenth century, many men and women also died in the prime of life; some of those headstones contain tantalizing clues about the people themselves, leading one to wonder and speculate. An obelisk memorializes Samuel J. Redfield, MD, who was born in Bainbridge, New York, in 1833 and died in Copper Hill, Michigan, in 1864; his infant son, Samie J., who died in 1861, is buried beside him, but Mary, the wife and mother, is absent. Did Samuel never recover from his son's death? After her baby and husband died, could Mary no longer bear to remain in this isolated hinterland, and did she then return home? Did she ever remarry and have other children? Where is she buried?

The modern gravesites are no less intriguing and affecting. The marker for Muriel Arnold, who died in 1964 at age 38, states matter-of-factly (but mysteriously as well), "She knew the secret of happiness." The headstones for Catherine Mussek, 1899-1996, and Clarice Mussek, 1933-1990, stand boldly and bravely by themselves. Were they mother and daughter? If so, then mother outlived adult daughter, always a sad fate. But what became of the absent husband and father? Two sets of wind chimes hang from a pine tree near the grave of Marcia Davis, who died in 2002 and whose husband's adjacent plot awaits him. Her epitaph—a short, modern prose poem, Carveresque in its terseness—reads, "You were here. You are loved. You made a difference." And a simple headstone marks the grave of David A. Lewis, MD, who died on September 12, 2001—the day after 9/11—of unstated cause. He was forty-three, and he left behind a wife and three young children.

After dinner that evening I join Marcia and some of the other guests around the fireplace in the Lake Breeze's common room. (Even in August the nights on the Keweenaw are chilly enough to make one appreciate a fire.) There I learn that my fellow guests, Midwesterners all, are longtime patrons of the inn who return year after year. One couple, from Menominee, Michigan, are avid bicyclists who come to ride the peninsula's scenic, hilly roads on custom bicycles that Chris, Marcia's partner, designs and builds. Another couple, in their midsixties, live in Saint Clair, Michigan, northeast of Detroit; the husband recently retired from Ford Motor Company after a career as an automotive engineer and test driver. The conversation soon turns to the history of the area, and I begin to gain a sense of the extent to which Ford's influence reached into the area. In the 1920s, as the copper industry was declining, Henry Ford purchased thousands of acres of timberlands and established a lumber mill and company town at the base of the Keweenaw Peninsula to produce wood for Model Ts. Although Ford originally came to the area for business reasons, he grew to love it: he built a commodious "cottage" for his family near Pequaming on Keweenaw Bay; he brought his friend Thomas A. Edison to visit; and he eventually became a member of the exclusive Huron Mountain Club, which owns and maintains a large private retreat along Lake Superior northwest of Marquette, Michigan. To this day the club remains a bastion of old Midwestern money, with membership held in large part by descendants of the founding members.

The wind, which has been light and variable for the past couple of days, overnight increases out of the northwest, and even in my room, which faces inland, I can hear, or feel, the big lake's swells pulsing on the basaltic boulders that form the inn's foundation along the water. I sleep well to the lake's rhythm, waking to a sparkling early-fall day, with a warm sun penetrating and tempering the cool air. I take a cup of coffee to the glass-enclosed porch overlooking the water. The wind has stirred the shallows to an aquamarine hue that darkens farther offshore, and the lake's surface explodes in myriad whitecaps. The couple from Saint Clair—Jack and Liz Speck—soon join me, and we spend the next hour chatting comfortably as the swells break on the dark, angular boulders below us—a percussion that resounds dully in my sternum—and the spray flies through the pellucid air, reflecting and refracting the bright sunlight.

Jack and Liz are wearing smart casual clothes and fashionable sunglasses and exude an air of prosperity, energy, and good health. Jack has a ruddy complexion and an outgoing personality, but he speaks in a soft, reassuring voice, without any of the bluster I expected. He grew up poor in Detroit, and although he is obviously proud of what he has accomplished in life, his manner is charmingly down-to-earth. They are a well-traveled couple, and Jack comments that the color of Lake Superior this morning reminds him of the tropical waters of Hawai'i, which he and Liz have visited several times. But he worries about the future of the Lake Breeze and other small businesses on the Keweenaw. Michigan is no longer promoting the Upper Peninsula as a vacation destination; the state's economy is in a shambles and unemployment is high; and many people in lower Michigan can't afford even the relatively short trip north across the Mackinac Bridge. Like many Midwesterners, Jack laments the steady decline of American industry and manufacturing; he sees no way that Americans can compete with cheap foreign labor, and it troubles him. I know little about these matters, which seem to me enormously complex, so I simply listen quietly.

When the opportunity presents itself, however, I ask him about something more personal: his work for Ford. Jack smiles, pleased that I am interested. In his quiet voice he then shares with me a few of his favorite stories: about driving cars at Ford's test facilities in Michigan and Arizona; about his acquaintance with the Scottish Formula One driver Jackie Stewart, who served for many years as a Ford consultant; and about several brief, amusing encounters with members of the Ford family itself. (Jack confesses that, much to upper management's dismay, he and several other Ford test drivers loved, owned, and drove Chevrolet Corvettes.) As he talks, I bask in the sun, enjoying his stories of a distinctively American life I never even imagined before this morning. Time passes quickly, and when Jack and Liz rise, announcing they need to get on the road home, I am sorry to see them go.

* * *

During the summer of 1913 tensions were high on the Keweenaw Peninsula. After members of the Western Federation of Miners voted in early July to strike if managers refused to meet with their representatives to discuss the workers' concerns, the local union sent the companies a threatening letter that the companies ignored. Wanting to take advantage of warm summer weather, the WFM called a strike on July 23, targeting particularly the area's most prominent company, Calumet and Hecla. That afternoon strikers wielding clubs and baseball bats marched on C&H and confronted and attacked men who were changing shifts. Although no one was killed, the governor ordered the Michigan National Guard to the scene, and the following day the companies suspended operations. That was a calculated move on the companies' part. They had stockpiled significant copper reserves and had set aside substantial cash to pay loyal, nonunion workers, and the mine managers believed that through a shutdown they could break the strikers' will and ultimately destroy the underfunded union. Quincy Shaw II—the son of the original Quincy Shaw—who had become president of C&H after Agassiz's death, told MacNaughton that although "it may seem hard on the better men, I believe that they and the Companies in the long run will profit most by a reasonably long shutdown." MacNaughton reported that the mine managers were "all of one opinion, namely, that the Union must be killed at all costs."

The strikers received encouragement or support from nationally known figures, including labor organizer Mother Jones, attorney Clarence Darrow, and Samuel Gompers, president of the American Federation of Labor. But the strikers' cause was hampered by the union's lack of financial resources and ethnic divisions within the strikers' ranks. The deepest rift developed between the skilled underground workers, mostly Cornishmen, Irishmen, Scots, and Scandinavians, and the unskilled workers, mostly Finns, Hungarians, and Croatians. The skilled workers had generally worked longer for the companies and felt more allegiance to them; they earned more money and had more to lose economically; and over time they grew suspicious of the militant socialism espoused by union officials and their unskilled coworkers.

In the middle of August the companies, sensing the divisions within the strikers' ranks, prepared to resume partial operations. By that time the state had recalled half the National

Guardsmen, and the companies hired private guards to protect company property and the men returning to work. On August 14 an altercation between private guards and strikers who were trespassing on company property escalated into the shooting deaths of two Croatian men, the strike's first martyrs. Those killings temporarily galvanized the movement and generated new financial support for the union from labor organizations across the country. September was marked by other violent confrontations. The companies, however, still refused to negotiate with the union. They rebuffed offers to mediate the dispute, hired scabs, and obtained an injunction prohibiting the strikers from harassing men returning to work. Through the fall, as temperatures dropped and the daylight faded, the stalemate dragged on. On a cold night in early December a local union organizer and several Finnish strikers fired shots indiscriminately into a boarding house, killing three Cornishmen who had recently returned to work and seriously wounding a young girl as she slept in her bed. Those shootings undercut the strikers' popular support and further exacerbated the ethnic divisions within their ranks. After nearly five months the strike appeared to be collapsing under the combined pressure of approaching winter weather, economic hardship, and ethnic mistrust.

To bolster its members' flagging spirits, the union decided to host a Christmas Eve party for the strikers' children at Red Jacket's Italian Hall, a two-story building owned by the Societa Mutua Beneficenza Italiana. The society leased the first floor of the two-story building to a bar and an A&P grocery store; on one end of the building double exterior doors opened to a steep set of interior stairs that provided access to the building's second floor, which included a large meeting hall with a kitchen and an elevated stage. By the middle of the afternoon as many as 175 adults and five hundred children (some unescorted by a parent) crowded the upstairs meeting hall, singing carols and watching a Christmas pageant on the stage. A long line of children waited to visit Santa Claus, who handed treats to each child. Then, at about 4:30 p.m., a disturbance erupted. People, mostly children, screamed and began rushing down the stairs toward the exit. To this day no one knows what caused it. Some witnesses later said that a man shouted "Fire! Fire!"; some even said they saw the man who shouted it. At the bottom of the stairs the heavy exterior doors were closed; some witnesses later said they had been barred. People tripped and fell on the stairs, but the crowd behind them, in its panic to escape the building, continued to surge forward, trampling some who had fallen, trapping others against the doors. For a few minutes the victims' agonized cries would have filled the bitter twilight; all too soon it would have been over.

"People started dying from the bottom up," Larry Lankton wrote, "killed under the crush of their friends and neighbors, their brothers and sisters." In the end seventy-three people died in the melee, suffocating at the foot of the stairs. Sixty of the victims were children between the ages of two and sixteen; two thirds of the victims were Finnish. Rescuers removed the bodies to a temporary morgue set up in the town hall. Funerals were conducted in the local Finnish churches, and a massive funeral cortège accompanied the bodies to the nearby Lake View Cemetery, where they were buried, one by one, within view of Lake Superior.

Immediately afterward the union ill-advisedly tried to capitalize on the tragedy. Charles Moyer, the national president of the Western Federation of Miners, rejected money donated to the victims' families, declaring that the union would take care of its own, and publicly blamed mine managers for the disaster. Some union officials even went so far as to allege that mining-company agents had shouted "Fire!" and then barred the door. At a fundraiser in Chicago the WFM showed newsreel footage of the Italian Hall, the funeral cortège en route to the cemetery, and, most distressingly, the corpses of six little girls laid out in the temporary morgue.

The various witness accounts differed in crucial details, and neither a coroner's inquest nor a Congressional investigation was able to determine exactly what happened at the Italian Hall on that terrible night. Despite the tragedy, however, the tension that had gripped the Keweenaw since the previous summer slowly began to relax. The victims' deaths seemed to serve as a catharsis, draining the last of the violent emotions from the strike's exhausted participants. The victims were buried; the families grieved; time passed. Through the rest of the long winter the violence subsided. In early April 1914 the union, financially depleted, cut the strikers' benefit payments, and on Easter Sunday the remaining union members voted overwhelmingly to return to work. The people of the region seemed to want to forget the strike's ordeal, and the Christmas Eve tragedy passed quietly into history, slipping slowly beneath the surface. In the early 1940s Woody Guthrie wrote and recorded a song called "1913 Massacre," adopting the union's version of events, but it never became one of his standards. In her otherwise comprehensive 1944 treatise about Lake Superior, Grace Lee Nute didn't even mention the Italian Hall tragedy.

Breaking the strike did little to enhance the Keweenaw mines' long-term viability. Although they increased production and earned record profits during World War I, immediately after the war a number of factors—including fierce competition from copper mines in Arizona and Montana—combined to drive a stake through the industry's heart. Calumet and Hecla, the titan of the Keweenaw, outlasted most of its rivals, but after World War II even C&H was able to operate only sporadically. In 1970, more than a century after Edwin Hulbert discovered the rich conglomerate lode, its new corporate owner shut down the mine and turned off the pumps for the last time, and the underground passages began to fill slowly with water.

* * *

On my second day on the Keweenaw, as I am driving from Eagle Harbor to Copper Harbor, I take the scenic drive to the top of Brockway Mountain. The road, originally constructed as a public works project during the Great Depression, is a narrow, potholed affair that climbs steadily from Lake Superior's densely forested shore to the mountain's open, windswept summit ridge, more than seven hundred feet above the lake. As the road gains the ridge, it curves sharply to the right and I am surprised to see, standing exposed to the elements, a weather-beaten modular building named the Skytop Inn. A couple of dozen cars, RVs, pickup trucks, and motorcycles are parked along the asphalt road in front of the building.

Many people are standing near their vehicles, taking in the panoramic aerial view. From this vantage point, looking west, one can see the peninsula's verdant ridges curving south toward the mainland; the jagged black basaltic outcrops forming the small harbors along the peninsula's northwest coast; and, stretching across the horizon, Lake Superior's blue immensity. Like the others, I stand quietly for a few minutes admiring the view before deciding to look in the Skytop Inn. When I enter the building, I discover that it is simply an old-fashioned souvenir shop, and I am taken aback by the bustle inside. The interior is crowded with adults and children chattering excitedly as they pick through tables and racks of typical tourist wares: copper jewelry and knickknacks, polished Lake Superior agates, key chains and shot glasses, T-shirts, Minnetonka moccasins, kids' toys and games, postcards, and a few books by local authors. As is the case when I find myself in certain situations—stranded in a busy airport by a flight cancellation, for example, or involved in a heated argument over an inconsequential matter—I experience a sudden loss of motivation and purpose. (A friend describes it as "a sudden loss of cabin pressure.") My immediate reaction is to flee outside, but I am overcome by a powerful inertia and seem unable to move my arms and legs. And so I stand vacant-eyed in front of a postcard rack near the front counter, staring at nothing in particular, trying to gather myself.

As I am standing there, I become aware of someone watching me from behind the counter. She is an older woman—perhaps sixty-five—with a coppery complexion and long, fine hair, gathered behind her head by a clip, that flows like a quicksilver stream down her back to her waist. She is talking quietly to a young boy at the counter, but she is looking at me. Although her face shows her age—her skin is not as taut as it once was—she has well-formed features and piercing blue eyes whose color changes subtly from moment to moment, like the lake's surface on a sunny but cloud-dappled day. Despite the bustle in the store and the fact that she is the only employee, her demeanor is calm and unhurried. As the young boy leaves, she holds up a pair of binoculars and motions me over to the counter.

"Would you like to use these to look at the lake?" she asks softly as I approach. Her accent is German or Scandinavian—I'm not sure which. The air around her smells faintly of wintergreen.

"If you look toward the horizon, you can see Isle Royale. It's fifty miles from here. It stretches for a long way across the lake."

She passes me the binoculars. As I take them, she allows her hand to linger momentarily on mine. Her touch is cool, and there is no jewelry on her fingers or wrist. She is wearing leather sandals with socks, jeans, and a loose-fitting, lightweight woolen sweater. Although slender, she has a womanly figure, and when she turns for a moment to answer another customer's question, her sweater stretches across her body, revealing the lake-swell of her breasts. After she finishes with the other customer, she turns back to me.

"The ship that you can see out there now heading west is a saltie—one that came across the ocean. You can tell by the superstructure at the rear of the ship. Or so they say."

She is looking at me with some curiosity. Despite other people pressing around the counter, jostling each other to look at the merchandise in the cases, I feel as if she and I are enclosed in a private capsule that exists outside of this time and place. Our conversation, though not personal, somehow feels very intimate. I suddenly want to ask her about her life and how she came to be here, in this unlikely place at the end of the road. I feel as if she knows something about the land and the lake that she could teach me.

"Stay as long as you'd like," she says quietly.

And in that magical moment the other people in the store disappear, and the store itself disappears, and the vehicles parked outside on the asphalt road—and in my mind's eye I suddenly see the Keweenaw as it once was: a land of dark and mysterious forests filled with bears, moose, and wolves; of trout-rich rivers rushing and falling over outcrops of black basalt; of ridges where nuggets of pure copper lie miraculously exposed on the ground; of snow falling gently on dark winter nights; of Superior's mysterious thrum; of the world as it was in the beginning, before words were invented, and someday will be again—a world of natural beauty and quietude—world without end.

# # #

Princess Pine, Wisconsin: The Last Redoubt

> It was intelligence and nothing else that had to be opposed. Presumably that is why [he], who had the job, was armed with an immense intelligence.
>
> Søren Kierkegaard, *Journals*

The red log cabin known as Princess Pine lies deep within the Chequamegon National Forest in northern Wisconsin, on a bend of the East Fork of the Chippewa River. It is difficult to find; no signs point the way. The turnoff from Wisconsin Route 70 between Loretta and Winter is unmarked, and the anonymous two-laned roads through the national forest wander without apparent purpose or destination, intersecting other anonymous roads in dark, sylvan settings. If one didn't have detailed, precise directions, one could drive these back roads for a long time, following wrong turns to their inevitable dead ends, before finding the way home.

I always approach Princess Pine with a mixture of pleasure and trepidation, for I'm never sure whether I will find Peter in a jocular, light-hearted mood or a dour, acerbic one. Not that it really matters how I find him when I arrive: I know from experience that his mood will oscillate between those two poles at various times during my visit. A visit with Peter is like riding in a canoe with an expert paddler who, just when you're beginning to relax and enjoy the scenery, executes a deft midstream maneuver and intentionally brings the canoe to its tipping point.

* * *

Today is a bright, balmy September day in the Chequamegon, with the sun tracing its ecliptic across the southern sky and a steady south wind stirring and silvering the leaves on the trees. The air is warm, almost summery, but the season is illusory. Within the next month or six weeks the first cold front of the year will drop down from Canada, and the leaves will quickly change and fall. At this northern latitude summer is short, fall is fleeting, and winter is always lurking around the corner.

I turn into the driveway—a dirt-and-grass two-track that curves through a forest of red and white pines, balsam firs, hemlocks, aspens, and birches as it descends gently toward the river. There the cabin sits in a glade along the river's bank. I turn off the engine and sit in the car for a minute, relaxing after the four-hour drive from the Twin Cities. From this vantage point I survey the property: the cabin itself—tidy, quiet, seemingly deserted; the neatly stacked cords of wood (properly sized to fit the living-room stove); the bird feeders filled with sunflower seeds and suet; and the small, well-tended vegetable garden encircled by a tall, welded-wire fence. The garage door is open, and the Weber is outside. Two does and a fawn are browsing on aspen saplings outside the screened pavilion in the yard. The scene is idyllic: the little house in the big woods. Suddenly Peter looms up beside the driver's side window, startling me out of my reverie. I have no idea where he came from. He raises his dark, bushy eyebrows and widens his eyes in exaggerated surprise, as if he didn't expect to find me here. He is brandishing a grill brush and tongs. He looks demented.

I haven't seen him in a couple of years, and his face has aged. Once angular, it has filled out, and his cheeks are beginning to sag around his jaw line. He has shaved his beard and his hair is thinner and grayer than it used to be, but I notice that it is long and tied in a ponytail under his ball cap, as it was when I first met him almost thirty years ago. And although there are pouches underneath his eyes, making them appear even darker than they are, his irises are twinkling and filled with mischievous good humor.

I get out of the car and we give each other a brief man-hug, patting one another lightly on the back.

"It's about fucking time you got here," he says then. "Did you bring dinner?" He enunciates the words clearly and slowly, his voice slightly nasal, the rhythm of the sentences slightly sing-song. A distinctively Wisconsin accent. Northern Wisconsin. Partly authentic, partly put on.

Susan comes quietly out of the cabin, and we stand for a few minutes under the towering white pine in the front yard, getting reacquainted with each other as old friends do when they haven't seen each other in a long while. The conversation meanders pleasantly from my drive today to this past winter's weather, to a black bear that recently ambled through their yard, to national politics and current events.

"Welcome to your safe house in the woods," Peter says matter-of-factly, summarizing this last topic. "As civilization disintegrates, you are always welcome here."

* * *

Like most people worth knowing, Peter defies easy characterization. And yet, he is, in many respects, a product of his place and time. Born in Milwaukee in 1947, he seems representative of that ethnically diverse, politically progressive city on Lake Michigan. In the middle of the nineteenth century Milwaukee attracted thousands of immigrants—mostly economic refugees—from Germany, Poland, and other Eastern European countries. They ended their diaspora here, settling into tightly knit communities and taking jobs in the city's rapidly expanding industries (including its famous breweries). Because of the presence of that large working class, Milwaukee became a center for the progressive, labor-oriented politics that has long distinguished the Upper Midwest (or at least a significant segment of its population). During the first half of the twentieth century the city elected three socialist mayors (and remains the only major American city ever to have elected even one). Milwaukee's version of socialism was often referred to as "sewer socialism" because it emphasized practical matters, like the efficient provision of government services to its citizens, more than ideology. The city continued to grow and prosper through World War II before its industrial base began to decline in the 1950s, and white flight to the suburbs eventually produced a racially segregated inner city that struggled through the later decades of the century.

Peter was born here to a German Lutheran father and Polish Catholic mother, attended public schools in the city, and came of age during the social and political turmoil of the late 1960s. He adopted the era's countercultural lifestyle—sharing communal houses with friends, dropping in and out of college, playing his acoustic guitar in local coffee houses—and became a political activist. While attending the University of Wisconsin at Milwaukee, he became a prominent figure in the campus movement against the Vietnam War; when his student deferment ended, he applied for conscientious objector status; and in November 1969 he and Susan rode a bus to Washington, DC, to participate in the antiwar march on the nation's capital. And then something happened. I'm still not sure what. But he gradually became disenchanted with the cause. Perhaps he recognized the naïveté (or intellectual limitations) of his fellow protestors, or perhaps he simply tired of the fight. I tend to think that his maturing intelligence displaced his youthful idealism and that a certain fatalistic streak in his personality—one of those things that seem integral to the person I know today—began to color and dominate his worldview.

He and Susan had married in October 1969, and a month later she was pregnant with their daughter, Anne. Peter dropped out of college for good and took a job in a leather tannery located along the Milwaukee River just north of downtown. He worked at the tannery for more than twenty-five years, eventually becoming a shift foreman and then the plant's quality-control manager. He was working there when I met him in the early 1980s, and he, Susan, and Anne were renting an old clapboard house in a nearby working-class neighborhood. During my visits I sometimes accompanied him to the plant after hours or on the weekend to check on the security of the building and the progress of various orders. The tannery had been constructed in the nineteenth century of local Cream City brick, but its exterior was discolored by years of dirt and grime, and its interior was vast and cavernous—cold and drafty in the winter, poorly lighted no matter the season, and filled with open vats of noxious, vile-smelling chemicals for depilating, tanning, and dyeing hides. Mingling with the chemical smells was the unmistakable taint of organic decay and death. It was a relic of Milwaukee's industrial past, and it would soon close its doors as its business migrated overseas to countries with cheaper labor and less stringent environmental regulation.

For a few years after the plant closed Peter consulted with other tanneries in the United States, Canada, and Mexico, but that work eventually disappeared as well. Meanwhile, Susan had returned to school to earn a nursing degree and was working for the city in its public health department, responding to outbreaks of infectious diseases. But by the mid-1990s, now well into middle age and with Anne grown and out of the house, they decided they were ready for a change. They began to take weeklong trips to northern Wisconsin to look for property where they could escape the city's noise and congestion. In 2000 they bought the cabin and eight and a half acres of land, calling their retreat Princess Pine after a rare club moss, resembling a miniature pine tree, that grows in the area. I had thought that they were intending to spend only long weekends and vacations at the cabin, but in 2005 they left their house in Milwaukee with Anne and her new husband and moved north to live here full-time.

And it is here, in the middle of the North Woods, in the middle of nowhere, that I come every couple of years to renew our friendship, to experience Peter's intelligence and skewed sense of humor, and, as has long been the case with my visits, to restore my sanity.

* * *

I met them when they were visiting the small, remote national park in the American Southwest where I worked in the early 1980s. Susan and Anne came into the visitor center while I was staffing the information desk, and we began to chat. Both had creamy skin and long, fine brown hair, and both were wearing jeans and T-shirts. Anne was ten years old and appeared tomboyish in a Milwaukee Brewers baseball cap; Susan's hair hung to her waist, and she looked so young that for a few minutes I thought they might be sisters. They seemed to be sweet, wholesome Midwesterners, and I was surprised, to put it mildly, when Peter joined them a few minutes later. He was wearing round, tortoise-shell glasses of the kind favored by East-Coast intelligentsia; he had a long, scraggly beard; and his hair, like Susan's and Anne's, hung to his waist. He looked like a Trotskyite member of ZZ Top. Although they were an unusual-looking family, it wasn't long before I began to sense a certain shared familial worldview: an intellectual curiosity that manifested a deep-seated skepticism; a wry, acerbic sense of humor. They asked intelligent, probing questions about the prehistoric Puebloan culture that once flourished in the area, and they delighted in silly word play and in questioning (and occasionally mocking) the more officious employees and overly bureaucratic rules that governed the park. Peter set the tone, but Susan and Anne gleefully (if quietly) contributed.

"When Ranger Rick"—his real name, by the way—"came by our campsite last night, he was wearing his gun. Does he always do that, or does he just think we're dangerous?"

"That female ranger with the ruby-red lips—the one from New York—told us not to walk along the path behind the visitor center, because—and I quote—'the snakes might be out of their holes.' We told her we liked snakes, so that was fine with us."

They camped in the park for almost a week, and at some point during that time I began to visit them at their campsite and to appreciate their skewed worldview. Part of the attraction for me was perverse: Peter's sardonic observations—unexpected, direct, occasionally aggressive—knocked me off balance (sometimes to the ground) and unsettled me. His view was contrarian, critical (in the scholarly sense of the word), vaguely Marxist. He challenged my bland assertions about the world, questioned my inherited, middle-class assumptions, and probed my untested philosophical tenets. In an intellectual sense he wouldn't let me get away with anything.

"You only say that," he said once, "because of where you grew up. If you had grown up on the south side of Chicago, your worldview would be considerably different. Not to mention your vocabulary. And probably your ability to use a knife or gun."

And yet—how can I explain this?—I sensed that his criticism wasn't malicious and that for some reason he was interested in my view of the world, and in me as a person. For several years they returned to the park each summer, and a bond slowly developed between us. I began to visit them in Milwaukee in the fall, after my seasonal work at the park had ended; and later, after I had started graduate school at the University of Iowa, I drove from Iowa City to Milwaukee at least once a semester for a break from the cloistered (and claustrophobic) academic world in which I found myself.

At that time both of us were avid runners—Peter had taken up running in his thirties to cope with the frustrations and stress of his workaday life—and we enjoyed long, slow runs along the lakefront and through the nearby neighborhoods. We ran in the mornings, which in the fall and spring are often damp and chilly in Milwaukee, so in my memory we are always wearing hats, gloves, and windbreakers. We ran on city sidewalks and streets and on short trails through the hilly lakefront parks, our breath condensing in vaporous clouds around us. We ran without talking, the only sounds, apart from the early-morning hum of the city, our labored breathing and the slap-slap of our feet on the pavement or ground. I was content, as I think Peter was, with the mindless repetition and wordless camaraderie of our physical activity. (Before age and deteriorating joints forced him to give up running, Peter ran more than a dozen marathons, including Boston and New York, recording a string of times around three hours.) Later Peter and Susan taught me to cross-country ski, and several times I flew into Milwaukee and we drove north for long weekends of skiing in northern Wisconsin or the western Upper Peninsula of Michigan, where I experienced for the first time the solitude and beauty of the North Woods in winter. (Peter was an excellent—and fast—cross-country skier and competed numerous times in the American Birkebeiner between Cable and Hayward, Wisconsin, North America's largest cross-country-skiing race.)

Those visits were stimulating in other ways as well. As a result of Peter's work in the tannery—where, as he said, he dealt every day "with the rotting flesh of the dead"—he and Susan had become vegetarians. They shopped for specialty food items at the local coop, and their kitchen was a bazaar of exotic cheeses, crackers, olives, dried fruit, relishes, chutneys, and preserves. During those visits we often went out to dinner—they always insisted on treating me, their wayward friend—sampling Milwaukee's many ethnic restaurants. (Whenever I tried to treat them or even pay for myself, Peter rebuffed my offer, saying dismissively, "Don't worry about it. It's only paper.") We ate the food of their heritage—German and Polish—as well as Italian, Greek, and Vietnamese, and it became a tradition, each time I visited, to drive south across the Interstate 794 bridge to the Three Brothers Restaurant in Bay View, where we drank stout Serbian beer, ate spinach burek and other Serbian specialties, and listened to strange Balkan music.

Their taste in all things was eclectic. They listened to music ranging from classic Italian and German opera to contemporary "World Music," and they decorated their house—an old, ramshackle affair with leaky windows and creaky wooden floors—with Hmong tapestries and inexpensive folk art from around the globe, purchased at ethnic fairs in Milwaukee. The house smelled faintly of sandalwood, and every room contained tidy shelves or stacks of varied reading material: the Bible, the *Gnostic Gospels*, the *Bhagavad Gita*, the Koran, and books about Zen Buddhism; the *Illustrated Oxford Dictionary* and various foreign-language dictionaries; *Howl* and *A Coney Island of the Mind*; *The Unbearable Lightness of Being*, by Milan Kundera, and *Do Androids Dream of Electric Sleep?*, by Philip K. Dick (long before the release of the latter novel's film adaptation, *Blade Runner*); *Wisconsin Death Trip*; the Foxfire books and various Audubon field guides; *How to Stay Alive in the Woods* and *How to Build a Wood-Frame House*; issues of the *Utne Reader*, *The Sun*, and *Silent Sports*. On Saturday afternoons we watched B movies on television (or, in later years, *Mystery Science Theater 3000*), and on Sunday mornings Peter subjected us to the most brazen televangelists of the era: Jimmy Swaggart, Jim and Tammy Faye Baker. Peter watched with rapt attention, occasionally mimicking their bombastic delivery and overblown rhetoric or offering caustic commentary, until finally Susan, Anne, and I could take it no longer and got up and went into the kitchen to drink coffee or tea and eat Danishes.

In one way, however, those visits were always uncomfortable. To save money, Peter and Susan kept their house cold, and in the winter the indoor temperature usually hovered around 55°F. Watching television in their living room, I sat with a blanket over my lap, wearing a midweight coat. I slept on a futon on the floor of a small room at the top of the stairs, wool socks on my feet, a knit cap on my head, and a sleeping bag draped over my torso and legs for warmth. Going to the bathroom in the middle of the night was a shivering, hurried affair. Strangely, though, I slept better there than anywhere else—a deep, restful sleep filled with vivid, evocative dreams that seemed to discharge the psychic voltage of my life. For me those visits were deeply therapeutic. I tend to be an introverted, inhibited guy, and somehow the proximity of my good friends— genial but edgy—and the mild physical discomfort of those visits seemed to undermine and breach the dam that normally held my psyche in check. For a couple of days the river flowed freely.

We are older now, all of us—much older—and Peter and Susan have moved far from the city, but in many ways my visits feel the same. I sleep on a futon in the living room, and the cabin is always chilly. Because of its remote location, it has no television reception, but in the mornings we listen to WOJB, the local National Public Radio affiliate, and in the evenings watch videos of old movies or television specials (often ridiculous ones, like "Elvis: Aloha from Hawaii") that they have borrowed from the library or bought at local yard sales. Occasionally we drive to the highway or a nearby lake to eat dinner at a roadhouse or supper club. And I seem to relax and breathe here, in the middle of the North Woods, in the company of my old friends, as I do nowhere else.

* * *

Peter thinks a lot about death, and his mood can be saturnine. During his life he has experienced his fair share of it. His father died suddenly when Peter was a young man, and his younger brother, Phillip, died of brain cancer in 2002, at the age of 48. Both of those events affected him deeply. At the same time, I'm not sure that they fundamentally changed his personality. Rather, I think that they reinforced his natural temperament, which is pensive and, to a degree, melancholic. He has always been interested in the larger philosophical questions and in what William James called the varieties of religious experience, and he has long applied his considerable intellect to pondering the existential mysteries of our time here on earth. One of the things I respect most about him is the brutally clear-eyed way in which he approaches those serious and daunting subjects. When I think of him, I am reminded of a famous quotation by Rainer Maria Rilke:

That is at bottom the only courage that is demanded of us: to have courage for the most strange, the most singular and the most inexplicable that we may encounter. That mankind has in this sense been cowardly has done life endless harm; the experiences that are called "visions," the whole so-called "spirit-world," death, all those things that are so closely akin to us, have by daily parrying been so crowded out of life that the senses with which we could have grasped them are atrophied. To say nothing of God.

Over the years Peter and I have discussed such subjects only rarely in a direct, serious fashion, but we often approach them obliquely, through humor. His sense of humor can be sophisticated or sophomoric, eschatological or scatological—he enjoys both high and low—but it always tends toward the dark. Nonetheless, its product can be more than a little amusing. In the mid-1990s, when he and Susan bought a house in an older neighborhood in southeastern Milwaukee, he sent me a copy of the real estate listing with the following handwritten note on the back:

This is the [new] homestead. The extreme quiet of this area is like death itself. The only constant sounds come from the wheezing lungs of the aged residents. The smell of cut lawns mingles with the odor of unknown medicinal balms used regularly, I think, by the neighbors. The only noisy life forms are birds and insects. All this will change when Anne and Bob move in.

P.S. We are only 1½ blocks away from Lake Michigan, where last week a person jumped off of a boat to retrieve his hat. The body has not been found.

At other times, however, his worldview produces something blacker, something born of frustration or anger, something designed, I think, to shock and discompose. Each morning during this visit, for example, he informs me that he needs to listen to the news "to find out if Obama's been assassinated. Because it's going to happen." On rare occasions over the years I've also seen him treat people with undeserved harshness. And, despite his intellect and better nature, he can lapse into adolescent sarcasm. Some years ago he submitted a fraudulent entry to a children's art contest in Milwaukee on the theme of "What Christmas Means to Me." Peter's entry consisted of an elaborate cartoon reminiscent of an underground comic from the 1960s: it showed a stigmatized Jesus bayoneting a surprised, skeletal Santa Claus, as rats scurried out of Santa's dropped bag. Overhead a wide-eyed Muhammad floated on a carpet, observing the carnage, and higher in the sky an anthropomorphized sun and moon indulged in an "astrological tongue kiss." On the form he listed his name as Peter the Disciple.

* * *

In addition to his other talents, Peter is a self-taught musician, and a good one. In college and as a young adult he played acoustic guitar, but over the years, as the demands of his life increased, he played less and less. In recent years, however, as he has found himself with more free time, he has returned to music, this time to an instrument—the accordion—that seems better suited to his idiosyncratic personality. Invented in Austria in the early nineteenth century, the accordion became an important instrument in Eastern European oompah and polka music and was popular among the German and Polish immigrants who made their way to Milwaukee in the nineteenth century. It reached its peak popularity in this country in the 1950s and early 1960s, when thousands of boys took up the instrument in the hopes of becoming the next Myron Floren, the famous accordionist for the Lawrence Welk Orchestra. But societal changes and rock and roll doomed it, and it soon became a novelty instrument played by a decreasing number of aging aficionados or younger musicians whose incorporation of it into their repertoire was largely ironic.

Peter's attraction to the instrument is not in the least ironic. Perhaps because of his German and Polish heritage, he has an emotional affinity for it. Because he also has a natural curiosity about the way things work, he was not content simply to learn to play the instrument. He bought an old accordion, disassembled it, cleaned the parts, replaced the reeds, and reassembled it. He studied the science of its sound. During the last few years that he and Susan lived in Milwaukee, he ran a thriving accordion-repair business, and he began to buy, rebuild, and resell the instruments. At one time more than fifty accordions were scattered around their house. He also learned to play traditional folk music from Eastern Europe, and he began to visit nursing homes in the Milwaukee area to give free concerts for the residents, who, Susan relates, sometimes became teary-eyed as they recognized the vaguely remembered sounds and songs of their faraway homelands.

* * *

I don't want to give the impression, however, that my visits are all darkness and gloom, because they're not. They always include many moments of lighthearted and creative mind- and word-play. Peter, for example, has a knack for nicknaming people and things, both those he knows well and those he doesn't. Years ago he began calling me "Flambeau," a moniker begat in irony—I am so not a Flambeau—that has become a term of endearment. On this trip he has already christened my wide-bodied rental car the "Hyundai Mama-san," and a couple of days ago, after we encountered a smug, professorial-looking middle-aged man with his much, much younger girlfriend (one of his students perhaps?) at a nearby state park, Peter immediately began referring to him as "Johnny Jump-up," an appellation that perfectly (if inexplicably) captured and skewered its subject.

My visits also often include innocent verbal or social pranks. When Anne was in junior high school, one of my visits to Milwaukee coincided with parents' night at her school. That evening I accompanied the three of them to her classroom, where I met Anne's teacher and where Peter introduced me, without warning and with a completely straight face, as Anne's "real, biological father." The teacher laughed nervously, but Peter didn't elaborate or explain, and Susan and Anne, standing nearby and smiling sweetly, didn't either. And little adventures or outings: on one of my previous visits to the cabin Peter and I donned swimming trunks and waded into the Chippewa River on a warm summer day, eventually floating on our backs and paddling slowly upstream over a deep hole, where Peter warned me, belatedly, not to dangle my feet in the murky water because of the large snapping turtles. And on another visit we toured the Fresh Water Fishing Hall of Fame in Hayward, Wisconsin, where we spent an hour on a misty, blustery fall day photographing each other in ridiculous poses in the mouth of the hollow concrete fish that the museum proudly advertises as "the world's largest muskie."

On this particular visit we take a day to drive to Superior, Wisconsin, to visit the Harrington Arts Center and A World of Accordions Museum, owned and operated by a woman named Helmi Strahl Harrington. Helmi herself is a latter-day character: a musicologist with a PhD from the University of Houston who has devoted her life to this most peculiar musical instrument. Her arts center and museum is a world unto itself, occupying an old Presbyterian church in downtown Superior that she purchased in 2002, where she hosts accordion recitals in the former nave and in whose basement she displays, in an organized but bewildering manner, more than twelve hundred accordions and more accordion memorabilia than one would have ever thought existed. Peter donated most of his accordions and accordion parts to the museum, and when we arrive today, Helmi greets us like long-lost friends. Peter is patient and gracious as she insists on updating him at great length about the world of professional accordionists, which I know doesn't interest him in the least, and showing him her latest acquisitions. He seems almost embarrassed by the attention she showers on him, and as I watch him interact with her, I remember that he is capable, when the situation requires it, of a quiet, understated manner that is really quite charming. The boy has manners. When the situation requires it.

* * *

No longer able to run, Peter has become an inveterate walker. Every morning before breakfast he takes a vigorous six-mile walk out and back along the hilly paved road toward the highway. When I am visiting, I often accompany him on these walks, which usually last about an hour and a half. We watch for wildlife and signs of wildlife; we observe the subtle, day-to-day progression of the season; and we talk. (One advantage of walking over running is that one can actually carry on a normal conversation.) Our conversations wander from subject to subject, visiting politics, current events, personal history, literature, and movies. Even his casual conversation is rhetorical in the classical sense of the word—replete with hyperbole, metaphor, irony, inflection, invective, and recurring verbal motifs. Peter loves to riff, and he is good at it. This morning, after listening to the news on the radio—grim dispatches from Iraq and Afghanistan and dismal reports of the United States' deteriorating economy—he is, not uncharacteristically, in a pessimistic mood.

"The world is winding down," he says matter-of-factly, enunciating his words slowly and carefully. "We're seeing the end of nature. We're seeing the end of constitutional democracy in America. We're seeing the end of quality ways of life."

He pauses for a moment.

"And the government, which should be helping people, is allowing, or even abetting, the decline. The federal government has become the tool of whoever happens to be in power. The cabal of the moment. The Republicans are probably more evil than the Democrats—they're motivated more by money and greed—but the Democrats are feckless. And they're capable of some real stupidity. So we have a choice after all: cupidity or stupidity.

"That's one advantage of living here. Up here you can pretty much ignore what the government is doing. If a government agent came onto your property, you could just shoot him and bury him in the woods. And no one would ever find him. Or care if they did."

I ask him if he misses the stimulation of living in the city.

"No," he says quickly and definitively, which surprises me, since I still think of him as an urban creature, and I've always assumed that he and Susan would eventually return to the city. But I could be wrong about that.

"Besides, the city isn't so much stimulating as assaultive. Everybody's always screaming in your face, 'Look at me! I'm special!' It's pathetic. And exhausting. . . . Fuck that noise."

We stop in the road, which runs straight for a long way in each direction. There is no traffic. "Listen," he says, and for a minute we listen without speaking. The only sounds we hear are the twittering of a few songbirds in the dark northern forest and, in a nearby wetland thick with tag alders, something—a beaver tail, perhaps—slapping the water. Then: "And the air up here is clean. It's Canadian air. Smell it this morning. Balsam fir . . . Forest duff . . . This is the smell of life on earth. This is better than anything in the city. Now, when I go back to the city, I can barely stand it. The traffic, the noise, the smells. The offal, it's awful."

We walk again for a few minutes in silence before he continues.

"There's idiocy here, there's idiocy there. They're just different kinds of idiocy. Up here, people are either real liberal or real conservative. You never know which. But I don't ask them about their political views. I might need their help sometime, so I just try to get along with all of them. Or at least stay on speaking terms. I need to preserve my options. Live and let live. As long as they're willing to help me plow the driveway in the winter, I don't care what their politics are."

Last year a young lesbian couple from Madison bought land near the highway and built a small cob house on it. They moved into the house and settled in as members of the rural community; one of them began working at the local food coop in the town of Winter. But the county discovered that they were using a composting toilet, not a county-approved septic system, for their domestic waste and threatened to condemn their house. The neighbors rallied to their defense, turning out to support them in a hearing before the zoning and conservation department, and the county eventually granted them an extension of time to come into compliance—a small victory for populist democracy.

"Up here, in some ways it doesn't matter what you believe. If the government is being stupid—and it doesn't matter whether it's the county, state, or federal government—everyone comes together to fight it. Governmental stupidity unites the people."

Suspicion of large organizations and institutions is one of Peter's characteristic traits (and something else, I realize now, that I have learned from him). He and Susan have worked hard to put themselves in a place (geographically) and position (financially) where they do not need to interact with most of our society's larger institutions. They own Princess Pine outright, so they don't have a mortgage, and they don't owe anything on their vehicles. This year they have allocated themselves an income of about thirty thousand dollars for living expenses. Their meager budget is motivated in part by an effort to preserve their retirement savings, but also in part, I think, as an experiment in living simply and frugally. They want to see how little they need, how little they can get by on. (When I think of their lifestyle, I recall Thoreau's exhortation: "Simplicity, simplicity, simplicity!") Although they would never describe what they are doing in such noble, altruistic terms, I know they are mindful that our planet has finite resources and that the less they use, the more they leave for others.

But in recent years Peter has developed serious health problems, including atrial fibrillation, that have forced him to interact with the American health-care industry more than he ever intended or wanted. And so he finds himself dealing with health-insurance companies and claims specialists a good deal of the time. Neither he nor Susan has employer-subsidized health insurance from their previous jobs, and this year they will spend about half their income to pay the premiums on their private health insurance, which, despite its cost, has a high annual deductible.

"And what do we get for all of that money? Some expensive tests, some expensive procedures, and a bunch of doctors who scratch their heads and say they don't know what to do. Oh, they're nice enough, all these young doctors. But they might as well bleed you."

Last winter, after his a-fib diagnosis, he was admitted to a hospital in Duluth for a procedure known as a cardiac ablation—a scoring of the heart muscle—which sometimes resolves, or at least alleviates, the condition. It was unsuccessful. So now he is on a strict diet and a drug regimen that, like all drug regimens, has its share of unpleasant side effects. The long-term prognosis is uncertain. Some nights his arrhythmia wakes him, and he gets up and sits quietly in the darkened living room, breathing slowly and deeply, waiting for his heart to calm. Nighttime meditation and morning walks provide some structure and predictability to his life, and a balm to his condition. But his own mortality is much on his mind these days. If anything, his condition has sharpened his already acute mind (and sense of humor). As Samuel Johnson observed, the prospect of death wonderfully concentrates the mind.

"My long-term health-care plan fires .22-caliber longs," he says dryly. "I've told Susan that if I get really sick, I'm going to walk out into the woods and blow my brains out, and she should just bury me where I fall."

I can think of little to say, because I understand and to some extent share his point of view.

His mother is currently in a hospital, supposedly the best in Milwaukee, receiving treatment for bladder cancer. Her treatment has been complicated by the sort of petty incompetence that seems increasingly common in all hospitals. The previous afternoon, as he was talking to his sister on the telephone, he referred to the hospital as "that grand, glorious failure," and a minute later he said harshly, "She should be getting better care. This isn't Guantánamo."

We pause to look at a baby wood turtle struggling through the grass along the road's shoulder, making its way toward the river. We give it a little help. Animals have always been important to Peter and Susan. Over the years they've owned, cared for, and doted on numerous household pets. And up here, in the middle of the North Woods, they place bird feeders around their property and, contrary to good ecological practice, feed the deer that venture into their yard. But they don't otherwise protect them, and they respect the natural order of things. Each year they may name all the does and fawns that eat the corn they scatter on the ground outside the cabin, but they understand that when one of them doesn't show up for a few days, they probably won't see it again. After all, timber wolves now roam these northern woods.

"Animals are more important than people," Peter says suddenly. "At least they're innocent. They're not malicious. They just do what they do."

He says nothing more; his last statement is the unexpected coda to our conversation. I recall a line from "Hurt Hawks," a poem by Robinson Jeffers: "I'd sooner, except the penalties, kill a man than a hawk." Peter often exaggerates for effect, but not now. He has simply stated what he believes, a succinct observation that hints at larger truths. As a species we humans unquestionably possess impressive intelligence and technological capability, but do we therefore have a right to do what we want, heedless of the consequences of our actions on our fellow creatures and the planet we share? Who or what has granted us that authority? But it is not only a question of morality and power; it is also a matter of our species' survival and sanity. If we don't begin to apply our intelligence more wisely—and by that I mean with more consideration for the planet's long-term health—then we will find ourselves, I fear, inhabiting a biologically depleted, barren world, one in which the only sound we hear is our own neurotic mewling.

Peter knows all this, and he has known it for a long time. And he has lived his life in stubborn but peaceful (if sometimes frustrated) opposition to the forces that are mindlessly and selfishly bringing it about. And if he dies without having stopped it—well, he won't be happy with that outcome, but I think he should be satisfied, because what matters in the end, for him as for the rest of us, is that he has fought the good fight, and that he has done so without compromising what he believes.

* * *

It is months later now—early spring the following year. Peter's a-fib is now "persistent," and his overall health increasingly unstable. The American economy continues to disintegrate, and the war in Afghanistan drags on. Over the winter Peter and Susan adopted a rescue dog named Bodhi—a middle-aged yellow lab with his own health issues—and Wisconsin Governor Scott Walker abolished public unions in the state.

I recently received the following email from Peter:

Flambeau,

"Primavera ekes its tendrils from beneath the latest winter dump and floes kerbang into the mushy shorelines, barely reaching the normal high water mark. Muddy puddles evolve from snow piles and mix with wild animal feces. We thank the gods for temperatures too low to make them volatile and prone to stinkiness." –

Pancreatitus

We have been attending the rallies and protests against the idiot fascist government of Wisconsin. It is just like the 60s except we are old. We hold signs and shout slogans that only we can hear. Hey hey. Ho ho. We are in solidarity with each other. Unified. I can go to Walgreens after the rallies to get my meds. It makes things really convenient. The dog comes with. The dog is a fascist. A Koch hound. I dress him like a lefty. What does he know. The calendar says spring but we are under snow except where the driveway and paths are plowed and there is ice and mud in those spots.

I played a gig at Julie's Trailside where Chef Siggi prepared some German Food. Susan stayed home with the dog, who is like an untrustworthy teenager that must be watched closely. I played popular favorites and Nazi music. The delicious food could not be consumed by either of us due to our peculiar dietary requirements. The fascist dog loved the knack and bratwurst.

We are back home from an extended visit to the south. My mother died and we attended to the aftermath. She was completing another round of chemotherapy when the miserable side effects took over. Interstitial bleeding caused her to bleed out. Her death certificate reads "Bladder

Cancer" as cause of death. No secondary cause was listed. I bought a camera with my inheritance. We brought her kitchen table and chairs home, too. I remember when my sister was tied to the chair with a dish towel until she finished some putrid meal. Memories.

I had been thinking about buying a used motorhome to travel to visit all of my far away friends. Gas prices. I will say no more.

I am still walking. Still walking = walking without movement? The dog has me doing 8 to 9 miles a day. He is brutal. I have gained 8 lbs over the winter. I can't figure it out.

Some days I feel OK. Some days I feel like shit. I have been short of breath the last few but it doesn't stop the death march. The dog needs the exercise. I am on an anti-depressant cocktail that seems to be working. I have no creativity and no traceable emotion. I am like Wimpy. Real laid back.

Susan has done all of the "wood work" this year, hauling the combustibles from the stacks to the stove. She did a lot of shoveling while yelling at me if I picked up a shovel. The many forms of impotence. We are still sharing the cooking and our menu is not varied but unquestionably delicious. 8 lbs. Susan is napping as I write this.

Please read this note quietly. She may still be asleep.

This is my communication to you. We miss hearing from you. We miss you. We want to know what is happening. Remember, when the government fails, you have a safe house in the woods.

Hope you are well.

Peter and Susan

I long ago stopped trying to understand and reconcile the seemingly contradictory aspects of Peter's personality: his harsh, sometimes bitter worldview and his personal warmth and generosity; his crudeness on the one hand and sophistication on the other. If we stop to examine ourselves, we will realize, I think, that each of us is a complex organism of sometimes-contradictory beliefs, emotions, and impulses, capable of thinking and acting, at times, with compassion and generosity and, at other times, with spite and pettiness. We are, each of us, a collection of pluses and minuses. The most that any of us can hope, for ourselves and for others, is that the good outweighs the bad and that our whole somehow adds up to more than the sum of our parts.

Like many people today, I work and live in a large metropolitan area. My life is busy—sometimes frenetic—and every day I am exposed to the relentless petty assaults of modern urban life: the traffic, the noise, the rudeness or carelessness of my fellow citizens. Some days I feel that I am nearing the end of my tether. More important, some days I feel that we as a society are nearing the end of something—the era of privilege and material wealth, perhaps, that many of us have come to believe we are entitled to. And it is then that I think about my friends in the north. I imagine flying to the Twin Cities and renting a car and driving to visit them in their red log cabin in the big woods; sitting with them in the twilight by the river and listening to the sounds of water riffling over rocks, frogs chorusing on the banks, and birds calling from the trees; talking about politics, literature, movies, or whatever comes to mind; and laughing quietly as the darkness slowly embraces us. And that prospect, that hope, often gets me through another day.

It is the gift they have given me.

# # #

Duluth, Minnesota: The Power of the Past

Home is where one starts from. As we grow older
The world becomes stranger, the pattern more complicated
Of dead and living. Not the intense moment
Isolated, with no before and after,
But a lifetime burning in every moment
And not the lifetime of one man only
But of old stones that cannot be deciphered.

T. S. Eliot, "East Coker"

Located at the western end of Lake Superior, in the middle of the North American continent, Duluth, Minnesota, has long had a dual personality. While it has always had strong cultural ties to the American Midwest, it is also, unexpectedly, a busy international port. Duluth faces Superior, Wisconsin, across the mouth of the Saint Louis River, and the two cities, sometimes called the Twin Ports, share a harbor protected from

Superior's storms and swells by a six-mile-long bay-mouth bar called Minnesota Point. Connected to the industrial cities along the lower Great Lakes by the locks at Sault Sainte Marie and the Great Lakes Waterway and to ports around the world by the Saint Lawrence Seaway, Duluth has long been a major shipping point for commodities from the American Midwest. In the early twentieth century it was, for a time, the largest port in the United States in terms of gross tonnage handled, and Duluth and Superior are still considered to be the largest freshwater ports in the world.

Like many other areas around Lake Superior, Europeans first settled the Duluth area in the late eighteenth century to facilitate the fur trade. At that time the area was known as Fond du Lac, or foot (or far end) of the lake, and both the North West Company and John Jacob Astor's American Fur Company established outposts there to stockpile furs extracted from the rich trapping areas in the continent's deep, cold interior. As the fur trade declined in the 1840s, the area was lucky: high-grade iron ore was discovered nearby, and mining rapidly supplanted the fur trade as the basis for the local economy. Large-scale logging and timber processing soon contributed to the economic mix. In the meantime, the locks at Sault Sainte Marie had been constructed, making possible large-scale shipping down the Great Lakes, and railroads connected the city to the rest of the Midwest. During the late nineteenth and early twentieth centuries Duluth boomed, and by the turn of the century it reportedly had more millionaires per capita than any city in the country (and is one of several cities often cited as the model for Zenith, the fictional city in *Babbitt*, Sinclair Lewis's satirical 1922 novel about social striving and conformity in American life). It continued to grow until 1960, when its population peaked at slightly more than a hundred thousand people.

But by that time the natural resources that had supported Duluth's economy were nearly exhausted. The nearby high-grade iron ore had been mined, and the old-growth forests logged. In 1981 the local steel mill closed, and Duluth began a precipitous economic decline that has been reversed only in recent years by its emergence as the commercial and medical center of a geographic area encompassing northeastern Minnesota, northwestern Wisconsin, and western Michigan and as a destination for tourists from other parts of the Midwest.

Today Duluth has largely remade itself into its new image: a picturesque town along the big lake that preserves and interprets its colorful past to attract regional tourists, while still serving as an important shipping point for Midwestern grain and lower-grade iron ore known as taconite. It is a combination that seems to be working, in large part because the town is indeed picturesque: Duluth's downtown, an eclectic mix of historic brick and stone buildings and modern concrete, steel, and glass ones, is strung along the lakeshore, while neighborhoods and parks occupy the hills that rise steeply behind it to heights of more than eight hundred feet, providing panoramic views of the city and its setting. And although the population of Duluth proper has declined since 1960, it is today the bustling center of the most populous metropolitan area on Lake Superior.

But it is a place that is beholden to its past and where the past is still palpable. And that is true for me in particular, because of my own family history. One of my great-grandfathers settled in Duluth in the 1890s—during Duluth's boom years—and established himself as a small-time politico and colorful local character, and I still have numerous cousins in town. The story of how one branch of my family came to be in Duluth is, I think, not exceptional. At the same time, because it is the story of my family, I find it inordinately interesting. It is also, I think, typical of an era in American history and is for that reason worth relating in some detail.

* * *

I know only the barest facts about Webster Eaton, my great-great-grandfather. He was born in Brighton, New York, near Rochester, on December 5, 1839, the son of Joel Eaton, a yeoman farmer, and Sarah Sibley Eaton, a Vermont native. In December 1861 he enlisted in the First Regiment, New York Light Artillery and served for three years during the American Civil War, fighting in some of that bloody epoch's bloodiest battles, including Second Bull Run, Antietam, Fredericksburg, Gettysburg, the Wilderness, Spotsylvania, and Petersburg. By the time he was discharged near Petersburg, Virginia, in December 1864, he had risen to the rank of sergeant.

One of my Duluthian cousins has an ancient document— tattered and fragile with age, held together with yellowed Scotch tape—that identifies itself as a "true copy" of Webster's discharge papers. (More precisely, it is an old, typed transcription of his discharge papers.) The information contained in that document is for the most part formulaic. It lists his dates of service and the engagements in which he fought and states that he was discharged "at Camp before Petersburg, Va., by reason of expiration of term of service." However, it also contains the following brief but curious biographical sketch:

Said Webster Eaton was born in Brighton in the
State of New York, is 25 years of age, 5 feet 9
inches high, light complexion, black eyes, brown
hair, and by occupation when enrolled a farmer.

In that brief description I am struck by the reference to "black
eyes." When I was growing up, my parents kept on their family-
room mantle a small, framed photographic portrait of Webster,
taken in Baltimore in 1862, showing a boyish man in uniform,
with thick, wavy hair and a serious expression suitable for the
time and occasion. His eyes do indeed look dark, but does
anyone really have black eyes? All I can say for certain is that
even in that portrait of the young soldier, one can see in his eyes
a certain resolve, a determination to make his way into the world
and leave his mark upon it.

After being discharged from the Army, Webster returned
to New York, married a woman named Frances Ames, and, for
reasons not clear from the historical documents I've found,
began migrating west, eventually reaching southwestern Iowa.
He was soon joined there by his older brother, Rice Eaton, also
a Civil War veteran. (Rice had served as a member of the First
Battalion, New York Sharpshooters and had been wounded in
the assault on Petersburg, where a Minié ball shattered his left
leg below the knee.) The years following the Civil War were a
time of rapid westward expansion and settlement in the United
States, and an era during which the publication of local
newspapers, encouraging and catering to the rush of
homesteaders to the vast open spaces of the American West, was
a profitable enterprise. Webster and Rice were of an
entrepreneurial bent, and together they founded and sold several
newspapers in rural counties in southwestern Iowa. Then, in the

early 1870s, after establishing the *Red Oak Express* in Red Oak, Iowa, the brothers followed the route of the Burlington and Missouri River Railroad west into south-central Nebraska.

At the site where the B&MRR joined the route of the Union Pacific Railroad, a new town, originally named Kearney Junction and later shortened to Kearney, was platted and incorporated. Here, in 1873, Webster established the *Central Nebraska Press*, a weekly newspaper, and soon began to diversify his business interests. To encourage the construction of the transcontinental railroads, Congress had granted the railroad companies millions of acres of public land along their routes, land that the companies were aggressively marketing and selling to finance the construction. (During that era the B&MRR and Union Pacific Railroad spent more than $1 million advertising land in Nebraska alone.) Kearney is located in the fertile Platte River valley, and in the early 1870s the combination of rich farmland and easy railroad access—aided by promotional advertising that intentionally understated the severity of the climate—lured thousands of hopeful settlers to Nebraska in general, and to the Kearney area in particular.

Kearney was and is the seat of Buffalo County, and some years ago I spent an afternoon perusing the public records in the basement of the county courthouse. I found numerous deeds listing Webster as grantor or grantee; through one deed alone he acquired more than 120 town lots. Writing in 1916, Samuel Clay Bassett, a local historian, provided the following explanation:

> It was understood that "Web" Eaton received, as subsidy to induce the publication of a daily at Kearney Junction, lots donated by promoters interested in the sale of city lots. This publication,

daily and weekly, served in an efficient manner, the interests of the city and surrounding country, taking rank as one of the leading papers of the state.

Mr. Bassett also observed that "'Web' Eaton . . . was a very shrewd politician; he secured by appointment, political preferment, and left the management of the *Press* largely in the hands of his brother, R. H. [Rice] Eaton." Years later, when Webster died, his obituary in the *Daily Hub*, the successor to the *Central Nebraska Press*, recalled that the *CNP* had been

> an aggressive [newspaper] and some of its editorials on matters of public interest when there was a big fight between the Union Pacific and the Burlington forces for making this a railroad point for both roads are said to have been strongly vitriolic. Many matters of like nature will be recalled by the old residents in which the *Press* was an active moulder [*sic*] of public opinion.

Webster appears to have been closely connected to the Burlington Railroad, and he worked briefly for the United States General Land Office in nearby Bloomington, Nebraska, along the Republican River, both of which may have provided him with opportunities to acquire more land. Whatever the means, he came to own a lot of it—land, that is—and apparently made a comfortable living in Kearney.

But Frances died suddenly in 1879, at age thirty-seven. After her death Webster remained in Kearney for only a short time before backtracking (literally) to Lincoln, the state capital,

125 miles east. (Rice stayed in the Kearney area, where he briefly managed the *Daily Hub*, served as postmaster, and later ran for Nebraska Secretary of State.) A year later he married a woman named Nellie B. Van Duzee. According to family folklore, Nellie was a granddaughter of abolitionist John Brown, but I now believe that wasn't true. (Although John Brown had a granddaughter named Nellie, she was born in 1878 and thus couldn't have been the Nellie B. Van Duzee whom Webster married in 1880. Webster would have been closer in age to John Brown's children—Brown had nineteen or twenty of them by two wives—but none of them was named Nellie, or Nell, or Eleanor. He had a daughter named Ellen, but she lived in California. Family stories usually have a basis in fact, but I haven't yet been able connect the dots on this one.) Webster lived in Lincoln for more than twenty-five years, where he served as assistant postmaster, established a pottery-manufacturing business with another brother, and was active in both local politics and the Masonic Order. But when he died in 1907, three years after suffering a "paralytic stroke," his body was transported back to Kearney and buried next to Frances's in the town cemetery.

During the trip when I searched the public records in the basement of the Buffalo County courthouse, I visited the Kearney cemetery and found Webster's and Frances's graves. I was in town in late August, and the weather was sultry. At midday the sun glared down, and the cornfields, which stretched to the horizon in all directions, writhed in the heat. Trains rumbled and clattered through town at all hours of the day and night, and countless grasshoppers chirred along the railroad tracks and in vacant lots on the outskirts of town, generating the ambient natural soundtrack of summer on the Great Plains. But there were also subtle signs of change. The leaves of the cottonwood trees along the river looked wan and fatigued, and the mornings were surprisingly cool and dewy. Autumn was imminent.

I drove to the cemetery one evening after an early dinner, when the sun was low in the western sky and the light oblique and liquid. The cemetery dated back to the town's early days and was spacious and park-like, with stately trees—oaks, maples, elms, and cedars—casting long shadows across the grounds. I spent a couple of hours there, and as the sun set and the light became crepuscular, I wandered from marker to marker, reading the inscriptions and wondering about the people who had lived and died in this frontier place. Then, in the gloaming, fireflies began to appear, animating the scene. They hovered and rose in the air around the tombstones, their abdomens suddenly lighting and just as suddenly blacking out—silent, winged creatures with soft, lambent lights—and as I looked across the quiet, darkened cemetery, there were hundreds of them, and in that mysterious time between day and night they seemed to be emissaries from another world, transmitting flickering messages from the past, signaling to me in a code I couldn't decipher.

· * * *

My cousin Dave was born in Duluth and has lived there all his life. He graduated from the University of Minnesota in Duluth and married another native Duluthian, and for most of his working life he and his older brother owned and operated a timber-brokering business that their father had founded. Although he is only nine years older than I, we are of different generations. Dave and my father were first cousins; my paternal grandfather and his mother were brother and sister. If I understand genealogical terminology correctly, that makes us first cousins once removed. Although I met his brothers and him when I was a small boy, as my family drove across country in 1959, I don't remember that encounter, and I didn't get to know him well until I was in middle age and beginning to do the research for this book. Since then we have become friends as well as relatives, and when I visit Duluth, I usually stay with Dave and his wife in their lovely lakeside home.

Like many Minnesotans, Dave is an old-fashioned outdoorsman, and although he is now approaching seventy, he remains an avid one. He hunts, fishes, hikes, canoes, sails, snowshoes, and snowmobiles. Until recent years Dave and a small group of friends took extended—I'm tempted to say "epic"—canoe trips every summer. As young men they started in the Boundary Waters, but as they became more experienced, they ventured farther north, seeking wilder water and country. One summer they put their canoes onto the Attawapiskat River in northern Ontario and paddled and portaged for a month, finally pulling their canoes from the water at the mouth of the Winisk River on Hudson Bay in Polar Bear Provincial Park. On that trip they traveled almost five hundred miles, filtered their drinking water from rivers and lakes, and fished for their dinner every night. The only human habitations they passed during the entire month were three remote native villages.

Although I would have loved to accompany Dave on one of his extended canoe trips, I never had the opportunity to do so. During one of my visits, however, we drove into northwestern Wisconsin, where he guided me on a daylong trip down the middle reach of the Brule River. The Brule is famous in this part of the world as a remnant of what once was: a free-flowing, spring-fed river of crystalline water, teeming with trout and other native fish, that flows and cascades from one pool to the next, all the while meandering through a pristine, forested valley, a large part of which is now owned and preserved by the state of Wisconsin. At least five American presidents—Grant, Coolidge, Hoover, Truman, and Eisenhower—have vacationed along the Brule. (Coolidge, having announced that he would not seek reelection, spent the entire summer of 1928 at the rustic Cedar Island Lodge, where a local Indian guide taught him to fly-fish and paddle a canoe. He also attended Sunday services at a small, whitewashed Congregational Church in the nearby town of Brule, where he reportedly listened attentively to the sermons of a blind lay preacher.)

The river also has deeper historical significance, as it is named after Étienne Brûlé, a young Frenchman who came to the New World in 1608, learned the Huron Indian language and otherwise adopted native ways, and served as one of Samuel de Champlain's interpreters. Although Brûlé himself left no written record of his travels, he probably explored parts of Lake Superior between 1615 and 1620 and may have been the first European to venture up the river that now bears his name. The man who usually receives credit for that accomplishment, however, is Pierre Greysolon Sieur DuLhut, the Frenchman for whom the city of Duluth is named, who paddled up the river in 1680, breaking through at least a hundred beaver dams, before portaging across what is now known as Brule Bog to Upper Saint Croix Lake, thereby "discovering" (i.e., becoming the first European to trace) one of the most important routes between the Lake Superior basin and the Mississippi River drainage.

When Dave and I paddled the Brule, I, an inexperienced canoeist, sat in the bow—where novices usually sit—while

Dave sat in the stern and expertly maneuvered us through the river's numerous twists and turns. We floated over three- or four-foot-deep pools where we watched cutthroat trout swimming statically against the current; saw river otters frolicking along the banks; and admired the lovely summer homes of the elite from the faraway urban centers of the Midwest: Chicago, Milwaukee, and the Twin Cities. It could have been 1620, 1720, 1820, or 1920—in all those years the river itself hadn't changed.

* * *

During the years when they lived in southwestern Iowa, Webster and Frances had three children: a boy, William Ames, born in Hamburg in 1866; a girl, Helen Merriam, born in Quincy in 1868; and another boy, Guy Arthur, born in Red Oak in 1871. Guy Arthur was my great-grandfather. Although five years separated the two boys, they were inseparable companions and, as they grew into adulthood, partners in adventure and business. Based on the photographs I've seen, they bore only a slight resemblance to each other—although both were handsome men, Guy Arthur was broader in face and body, while William Ames cut a more elegant, dashing figure—but they seem to have been kindred spirits and to have inherited from their father his wanderlust and entrepreneurial spirit.

Guy Arthur attended public school in Lincoln, Nebraska, but because his father had secured another temporary appointment with the General Land Office in Minnesota, he also claimed Saint Cloud, Minnesota, as his home. In the late 1880s Webster and the young Guy Arthur made a trip to Nova Scotia, apparently to investigate a possible mining venture, but it doesn't seem to have affected the long-term course of either man's life. Guy Arthur studied civil engineering at Claverack College in New York, graduating in 1889, and began to earn his living as a surveyor. In the early 1890s he and his brother worked as government surveyors in the Rainy Lake region in northern Minnesota. According to the *Commemorative Biographical Record of the Upper Lake Region,* a sort of *Who's Who* of the region published in Chicago in 1905 (whose entries were probably written by the subjects themselves), during their surveying trips the brothers "lived as long as eight months without seeing a white man outside of the members of their party. During one memorable trip they traveled forty-two days on snowshoes, camping every night." Their time in northern Minnesota coincided with a gold rush in the region, and the brothers staked a mining claim near Tower, Minnesota, where they built a log cabin.

The Minnesota Historical Society has in its archives several photographs of the Eaton brothers' cabin. One shows the interior of the cabin, with Guy Arthur, William Ames, and a younger, unidentified man posing in the cozy space. The cabin is furnished with a rustic table and chairs and a homemade bed, and a wood-burning stove is visible in the left foreground, its metal chimney vented through the cabin's pitched roof. The bed is neatly made with what appears to be a Pendleton blanket, on which a bloodhound, facing the camera like the three men, rests comfortably, its front paws draped over the side. Mounted on the walls are the accoutrements of the men's lives: rifles, a fishing net, and an animal trap; a pair of snowshoes and a wide-brimmed hat; makeshift shelves holding books, tools, and surveying instruments; and maps, postcards, and posters, including a cheesecake magazine illustration of a skirted cowgirl coquettishly revealing her bare legs below the knee—all displayed in a casual, almost artful manner.

Their mining enterprise didn't pan out, however, and the Eaton brothers soon traveled to Central America to ply their trade and pursue other opportunities. (Their father apparently helped finance the boys' various enterprises and schemes. My cousin Dave has a handwritten letter from Webster to Guy Arthur dated December 12, 1894, in which Webster summarizes some of their recent financial dealings, advises his younger son to "make haste to get here [to Lincoln] if you want[ ] to try for anything when the Legislature meets," and states that he "presume[s] Will is in Guatemala by this time.") The *Commemorative Biographical Record* contains this intriguing summary of the Eaton brothers' time in Central America:

> In 1895 the Eaton brothers went to Central America as part of the engineering force of President Barrios, to assist in surveying the line of the Guatemala Northern Railroad. Later they coasted along the Caribbean sea. During their stay in Central America they enlisted under Gen. Bogranz, the leader of a revolution in Honduras, but as the General was poisoned, the affair was abandoned.

After recovering from a serious illness contracted in Central America, Guy Arthur returned to the United States via Cuba and served for two years as the county surveyor of Wright County, Minnesota. There he met and married a woman named Jessie Belle Burton, and the couple moved to Duluth, where Guy Arthur and his brother went into business together. The historical documents I've found don't reveal the exact nature of that business, but it involved acquiring and either developing or selling mineral prospects and timberlands in northern Minnesota. The General Land Office's records indicate that in the early years of the twentieth century the brothers acquired thousands of acres of homesteads or failed homesteads in the region. How they financed those acquisitions is unclear.

Whatever the nature of the brothers' business, Guy Arthur, like his father, was active in both civic affairs and local politics. Again, the *Commemorative Biographical Record*:

> Like his father, Mr. Eaton has an inborn taste for political affairs, and he takes an active interest in the workings of the Republican party, at present serving as chairman of the 8th Congressional District Committee, which position he has held since 1902. He was largely instrumental in the election of J. Adam Bede to Congress. He is second vice-president of the Commercial Club, one of the leading social organizations of the city and a power in local commercial and civic affairs.

Another similar publication, the *History of Duluth and St. Louis County, Past and Present*, a two-volume, nine-hundred-page tome published in Chicago in 1910, refers to him as "among the leading spirits of Duluth" and summarizes his busy social-networking activities as follows:

> He is active in fraternal organizations, being a thirty-second degree Mason, a Knight Templar, a

member of the Mystic Shrine, the Knights of
Constantine, the Benevolent and Protective
Order of Elks, Knights of Pythias, the Modern
Woodmen of America, and the Independent
Order of Odd Fellows. He belongs to the
Commercial Club, the Kitchi Nadji Club, of
Superior, Wis., and the Duluth Boat Club, and
finds recreation in automobiling, yachting and
boating.

The overall impression one derives from these sources is of a
gregarious, socially ambitious, and financially successful
businessman with low-level political connections.

As a result, life in Duluth in the early twentieth century
was comfortable for the young Eaton family. Guy Arthur and
Jessie lived in a substantial house near the bustling downtown;
they moved in the small city's elite social circles; and they had
three children, including my grandfather, William Guy, born in
1900, and Dave's mother, Mildred Guy, born in 1906. (Another
boy, Richard Burton, was born in 1911 but died of cancer at the
age of sixteen.) Moreover, Guy Arthur's political connections
appear to have paid off: in 1906 President Theodore Roosevelt
appointed him postmaster of Duluth. My cousin Dave has a
caricature of Guy Arthur done at about this time by the political
cartoonist for the *Duluth News Tribune*. It shows an elegantly
coiffed man wearing fashionable boy's clothes sitting on the
floor in the corner of a room, with a toy boat named the "Jessie
B." nearby. A pie rests in the man's lap, and in his right hand he
holds an apple labeled "Duluth Postmastership." The caption
reads, "Little Guy Eaton / Sends you his greetin' / He has been

touching the pie, / He chucked in his thumb / And out came a plum. / Ah, what a brave boy is Guy!"

* * *

Although Dave and I didn't get to know each other until midlife, we like each other and have discovered that we share certain interests: in physically demanding outdoor activities, in history, and in American Indian culture. When I visit Duluth, even if I haven't seen him in several years, we fall into easy conversation and familiar camaraderie, like old friends. He is soft-spoken and possesses a calm, steady demeanor, and I now know him well enough to say that he has adopted, and embodies, a certain attitude toward the world in general—and the natural world in particular—to which I can only aspire: observant, tolerant, even stoic. He once told me that when he canoes or camps during mosquito season, he sometimes refrains from using Deet or other chemical repellents, instead wearing a simple head-net and trying to remain still and calm to avoid generating the body heat that further attracts the little pests: Zen and the Art of North Woods Survival.

Physically we bear little resemblance to each other; although we are about the same height, Dave is broad and muscular, while I have the wiry (to put it politely) physique of a longtime runner. But we have similar gaits, both of us tending to walk quickly and purposefully, with slightly exaggerated heel strikes. (I sometimes wonder if Guy Arthur, our common ancestor, strode through Duluth in the same manner.) And we both enjoy getting out into the woods. So when I visit Duluth, he and I often drive up the North Shore of Lake Superior and take a hike in one of the many state parks that today dot the lakeshore.

The North Shore is not only remarkably scenic but also rich in history. Near the town of Schroeder, for example, a granite cross marks the place where Father Frederic Baraga, a Slovenian Roman Catholic priest, and his Indian guide finally reached the shore in 1846, after paddling a birchbark canoe across more than forty miles of open water from La Pointe, Wisconsin, having survived en route a violent storm on Lake Superior. Frederic Baraga was, like Jacques Marquette more than a century and a half earlier, a figure legendary for his missionary work among the Indian tribes of the Great Lakes region. After coming to the New World in 1830, he worked first among the Ottawa Indians along the northeastern shore of Lake Michigan; then at La Pointe, where Marquette had also worked; then at L'Anse, Michigan, at the base of the Keweenaw Peninsula, where he established a new parish church; and finally, after being consecrated a bishop, at Sault Sainte Marie and Marquette, Michigan. During his years in the area he learned several Indian languages, compiled the first Ojibwe dictionary, and published numerous prayer books in Ojibwe. He was an intrepid, energetic man, visiting his parishioners—whether Ojibwe Indians or immigrant miners—regardless of season or weather, and, because of his common mode of winter travel, came to be known as the "Snowshoe Priest." He died in 1868 at the age of seventy, a venerated man, and is buried in a crypt beneath the floor of the Cathedral of Saint Peter in Marquette.

During one of my visits Dave and I drove along the North Shore to Tettegouche State Park, between the towns of Silver Bay and Little Marais, and hiked around Shovel Point. The hike is not long, but on the day we did it, an October storm was blowing across Lake Superior from the southwest, sending large swells crashing against the cliffs at the end of the point. The wind was fierce, whipping the water at the base of the cliffs into an aquamarine froth, and the spray occasionally showered us in our rain jackets as we stood on the trail admiring the lake's furious majesty. We were the only ones on the trail. Dave seemed transfixed by the scene, staring for long minutes into the wind and water, and I imagined him in the stern of a canoe in the middle of the lake, paddling resolutely into the tempest, guiding his small craft and its cargo across the dangerous waters.

* * *

In the early 1900s Guy Arthur was one of the principal organizers of the Minnesota Naval Militia, the naval counterpart of the National Guard, which the Minnesota legislature had authorized in 1899. He successfully lobbied the state legislature for funding to purchase textbooks, supplies, arms, and other equipment, and in 1906 he secured from the United States Navy, for training on Lake Superior, an outmoded 160-foot-long, steam-powered gunboat originally christened the USS *Fern* and renamed the USS *Gopher*. In 1915 a new armory for the Army National Guard and Naval Militia was dedicated in Duluth, a gala event attended by the Minnesota governor and other dignitaries. By the time the United States entered World War I in 1917, Guy Arthur had risen to the rank of captain. Called to active duty, he traveled to Philadelphia and was given command of the USS *Massachusetts*, a small, coastal-defense battleship that had been commissioned in the early 1890s. He later commanded the USS *Iowa*, a larger, newer battleship that had seen significant action in the Spanish-American War. Yet another publication of the era, *Minnesota and Its People*, provides this summary of his military service during the war:

> In the latter part of the war he had command of Division A of the Atlantic fleet, including the Indiana, Massachusetts and Iowa, and was the only officer not a graduate of Annapolis to be given command of a division of the Atlantic fleet. After the armistice he served on the staff of Vice Admiral Gleason. He was relieved of duty on July 10, 1919 . . .

What that summary fails to mention is the fact that during World War I Division A of the Atlantic fleet consisted of older ships deemed obsolete by the Navy whose mission was to provide training opportunities for naval officers and sailors as its ships patrolled the mouth of the Chesapeake Bay to deter incursions by hostile warships into the United States' coastal waters. But Guy Arthur seems to have taken his role in the Naval Militia seriously, and his accomplishments in organizing it and serving on active duty during the war are impressive. And his experience on active duty in the Navy during World War I seems to have marked a turning point in his life.

After World War I Guy Arthur returned to Duluth, where he continued to command the Minnesota Naval Militia, which by that time had evolved into a full-time job. He used his military connections to acquire from the Navy a new training ship, the USS *Paducah*, and during the summers led cadets on two-week training cruises on Lake Superior. His naval experiences undoubtedly influenced his older son, William Guy—my grandfather—to attend the United States Naval Academy, from which he graduated in the class of 1921. (My father, in turn, also attended the academy, graduating in the class of 1945.) And Guy Arthur's daughter, Mildred Guy—Dave's mother—enrolled at the College of William and Mary in Williamsburg, Virginia, in 1924, probably because the family had joined Guy Arthur in the Hampton Roads area during the war and she had become acquainted with it.

During this time the Eaton family continued to live comfortably in Duluth, although I have few details to relate. My father recalled a story about a gas explosion that severely damaged or destroyed the family's substantial house, but no one was injured, and what could have been a tragic affair was, in retrospect at least, the source of much family amusement. By this time Guy Arthur himself seems to have outgrown his youthful ambitions and to have settled into a comfortable middle age. His wife and children certainly loved and respected him—I know that by the affectionate way Dave's mother always referred to him. But Guy Arthur wasn't destined to live into august patriarchy. In April 1924 he developed a serious bacterial infection that targeted his kidneys and, following surgery in a Duluth hospital, succumbed to "acute nephritis with partial anuria." He was fifty-two.

* * *

Based on the photographs I've seen, Webster, Guy Arthur, and William Guy Eaton shared a strong family resemblance to each other. They were broad-faced men, with wide foreheads, thick noses, and full lips that turned down slightly at the corners when they weren't smiling—serious but not dour men. My cousin Dave shares their physiognomy, though his expression is lightened by a ready smile and a mirthful sparkle in his eyes. In other ways as well Dave seems the rightful heir of the line. He has always been something of an entrepreneur and free spirit. After his brother retired from the timber-brokering business that their father had founded, he continued to own and operate it on his own, riding the economic rollercoaster of the early 2000s with apparent nonchalance (though he later revealed to me that during the 2008 recession he and his wife had almost lost their house). And like his grandfather, he has always had an affinity for water, whether it is the Boundary Waters, the myriad lakes and rivers of central Canada, the Brule River, or Lake Superior itself. When he was growing up, his family often sailed on Lake Superior, and as a young man he regularly crewed on larger boats in the Trans-Superior International Race, a biennial sailboat race from Sault Sainte Marie to Duluth. I sometimes wonder if Dave inherited his affinity for water from Guy Arthur, if that particular personality trait is hardwired into his genetic disposition. Probably not. More likely he learned it from his mother, who in turn had learned it from her father. But who's to say exactly how or why we become the people we are, and whether a family tradition, practiced and quietly selected over generations, finally becomes encoded in our DNA?

To my eyes at least, I look little like Dave or our male ancestors. My face is long and thin, almost gaunt, and my nose straight and thin. When I was a young man, people often commented that I looked like a cross between my father and mother, and I think that was true at the time, when my father was middle-aged. Toward the end of his life, however, his face and nose broadened—the Eaton genes manifested themselves—and now, looking at photographs of him from that time period, I can clearly see his ancestors in him. Will the same happen to me as I age? And what else does my patrimony say about me? Although the men in my father's family were robust and adventurous as young men, their life spans varied. Webster had a paralytic stroke and died at age sixty-seven; Guy Arthur died of a kidney infection at age fifty-two; and my father suffered a debilitating stroke at age seventy-seven, although he survived in a diminished state for another eleven years. (His father, William Guy—my grandfather—did not die of "natural causes." He was killed in August 1942, during the nighttime naval battle off Savo Island, in the Solomon Islands in the South Pacific Ocean.) I am already older than Guy Arthur was when he died, and although I've always assumed that I would live a relatively long life—at least my biblically allotted three score and ten years—my longevity is not assured.

And what else do I carry within me as part of my genetic heritage, hidden and as yet unrevealed? What of other characteristics of my personality? My father seems not to have inherited Webster's and Guy Arthur's political inclinations or entrepreneurial spirit. He was a career naval officer, idealistic in outlook and dedicated to service to his country, and after he retired from the Navy, he taught science and math for twenty years in an urban high school for at-risk youth. Other than dutifully casting his ballot on election day, he had little interest in politics, and he wasn't motivated by a desire for wealth or acclaim. He was an altogether decent man, and when I was growing up, our family lived a comfortable but modest, and largely anonymous, middle-class existence.

And yet, even my father had a surprisingly independent, even rebellious side to him. In the 1950s, after he became a naval aviator, he flew P5M Marlin seaplanes in Panama with a racially integrated crew. (At the time he was the only pilot in his squadron, all of whom were white, willing to fly with a black crewman.) Later, when we were living in the Washington, DC, area and he was working in the Pentagon, he logged hours to maintain his pilot's qualification by flying up and down the East Coast on quasi-official missions of dubious purpose. When he flew south, he delighted in buzzing my maternal grandparents' house in North Carolina, cruising low over the pine trees and tipping his wings in greeting; and when he flew north to the naval air station in Brunswick, Maine, he always brought back crates of fresh lobsters for family and friends. He also had an inexplicable and irrational attraction to cheap but exotic cars. When I was growing up, he owned (among others) a Hillman Minx, a Studebaker Lark convertible, and an Opel Kadett— unreliable cars that often required him to spend the evening in the driveway with the hood up, working on the engine under a droplight, so that he would be able to drive to work the next day. He was a devout, churchgoing man, but he always enjoyed a well-mixed cocktail and was good-natured and loquacious (and often quite funny) after drinking a couple. We usually lived in bland, middle-class suburbs, and he was always viewed as one of the neighborhood eccentrics, the man who, for example, lit up the street with spectacular (and highly illegal) fireworks on July Fourth. The neighborhood kids loved him.

As for myself, as a young man I reacted, sometimes violently, against all that. I was a product of the era in which I came of age—the late 1960s and early 1970s—and I questioned everything my father espoused and believed in. When I was in high school, he and I often argued and, in my memory, went for weeks without speaking. I declined an appointment to the Naval Academy, choosing instead to attend a civilian college, where I majored in philosophy (choices that must have deeply disappointed him, though he said nothing). Despite all that, I realize now that I am in many respects his son, and always have been. I have little appetite for politics and little talent for making money. (I often wish I had inherited more of my great-grandfather's knack for turning a dollar.) And like him, I have always disdained the norm and rebelled against expectations. (I too feel compelled to swim across the current, if not against it.) As a young man I owned a series of oddball cars that required an inordinate amount of maintenance and repair, and if I have a choice between a popular brand or activity and a less popular alternative, I invariably choose, for no reason other than contrariness, the off-kilter. And, not surprisingly, I've always loved the smell of gunpowder on July Fourth. Although I spent my young adulthood as an itinerant, moving from place to place pursuing my idiosyncratic interests, I have a strong sense of civic duty and settled, somewhat belatedly, into a career as a civil servant. In the end, it seems, we return to our beginnings.

Toward the end of his life my great-grandfather sat in his dress blues for a photographic portrait. I don't know exactly when it was taken—only that it dates from the early 1920s, when he was about fifty—or what the occasion was. I've recently studied that picture. He was still a handsome man, especially in his uniform, with his captain's stripes on his sleeves and golden oak leaves on his cap bill. But his expression is not what I expected, knowing what I now know about his life and personal history. He looks appropriately serious for someone of his age and station in life sitting for a formal portrait—his posture is erect and his mouth is carefully composed in a neutral manner—but instead of the confidence or even hubris that I expected, his face conveys, more than anything else, an impression of kindness, shadowed, as his cap bill shadows his forehead, by an overarching sadness. Although his face still appears youthful and unlined, the hair on the side of his head is flecked with grey and his left eyelid droops slightly, suggesting weariness or some unknown disappointment or loss. I have no idea what lay behind and informed that expression; all I can say is that in this picture he looks like someone who had learned much from his experiences in the world and who, as a result, would be someone worth knowing and talking to. Although he died thirty years before I was born, in this picture he reaches out to me, silently and mysteriously, across the gulf of time.

* * *

During my last visit to Duluth, on a bright, brisk morning in late September, Dave and I drove to Forest Hill Cemetery to visit Guy Arthur's grave. Forest Hill is an old cemetery, dating back to the city's earliest years, and has long been the preferred resting place for Duluth's civic leaders. It is a lovely, well-tended place, with narrow lanes meandering among rows of graves that climb from a grassy field bordering a pond up a wooded, park-like hillside to a ridge overlooking the city and Lake Superior. On the weekday morning when we visited, the cemetery was nearly deserted, and all was quiet but for the groundskeepers' mowing and trimming activity, beelike in the distance, and, overhead, the occasional honking of a phalanx of geese headed south. The air, stirred by a light breeze, carried the faint, mingled smells of mowed grass and decaying leaves.

The Eaton family monument—substantial, stolid, and plain—is located in an older section of the cemetery on the hillside's lower slope, under a stately maple tree. Guy Arthur is buried there, next to Jessie, who survived him by forty-four years, dying in 1968 (and whom I must have met on that cross-country trip in 1959, when I first met Dave, though I don't remember her), and their younger son, Richard Burton, who died as a teenager in 1928. Small markers memorialize their older son, William Guy—my grandfather—whose body was never recovered from the waters off Savo Island, and his wife—my grandmother—who was cremated after she died in 1991 and whose ashes were scattered in the Pacific Ocean off the coast of California, to rejoin her long-dead husband. Dave's parents are buried nearby, across a small footpath from Guy Arthur and Jessie. On my father's side of the family this is the closest thing we have to an ancestral home.

Dave and I knelt for a few minutes beside the markers, weeding and brushing the debris from them. As we did, we talked about whether, when the time comes, we will be buried or cremated. Dave surprised me by saying that he doesn't like cemeteries and that whatever he decides to do, he doubts he will end up in Forest Hill. Although it's none of my business and I said nothing, I felt a little disappointed. All my life I've been a wanderer—a deracinated sort—and the thought that at least one branch of my family was rooted somewhere, was connected intimately to a particular place, and had maintained (and would continue to maintain) that connection through the generations— and, I suppose, through the ritual of burial—was comforting. But things change. These days more and more people are abjuring the formality of burial and cemeteries and the illusion of permanence they represent, making other arrangements for their final disposition, and the countryside is filled with graveyards that few people visit. In the end it matters more where we live, and how we live, than where our bodies lie.

And yet, as I write these words, I find myself hoping that whatever Dave decides to do, he will decide to have at least a marker installed there, in that lovely place, among our common ancestors. Although I long ago decided that I would like my body to be cremated and my ashes scattered in the mountains of the American West, in a particular place close to my heart, I also find myself thinking that I might request a spot in Forest Hill Cemetery, in Duluth, for a small marker—in that place on the shore of Lake Superior, which I've only recently come to know, that members of my family have long called home.

# # #

Acknowledgments

This book is a small one, but it took an inordinately long time to complete. After I started to work on it in the late 1990s, events large and small, global and personal, interrupted my progress. The United States endured the September 11 terrorist attacks and their long aftermath in Iraq and Afghanistan; my parents experienced difficult years of physical and mental decline before their final passing; several friends died too young after battling relentless diseases; my twenty-one-year-long marriage ended; and, finally, seeking some sort of renewal, I changed jobs and locations. Despite those interruptions and disturbances, however, I hope that readers find that the book possesses a consistent vision and voice.

As is the case with any long-term writing project, I couldn't have completed this book without the help of many people. During the early years when I was working on it, my former wife, Marty Daly, tolerated with good grace my numerous absences from our house and my domestic duties to travel to the Lake Superior region. During those trips, regardless of my original itinerary, I invariably ended up staying with my friends Peter and Susan Schultz in their red log cabin in the big woods in northern Wisconsin, where they generously provided me with food and drink, their familiar but stimulating company, and a welcome respite from the road. Similarly, when I visited Duluth, Minnesota, I often stayed with my cousin Dave Baumgarten and his wife, Penny, in their lovely lakeside home on London Road, where Dave shared with me his deep knowledge of his hometown, stories of our common ancestors, and copies of old family documents. He also introduced me to other family members and was always willing to take a day off work to show me his favorite places in the area.

Many years ago my friend Jay Everhart took a week out of his busy schedule to accompany me on the trip to Lake Superior's North Shore that launched this project. And various people—including Roberta Gable, Sam Dodson, Carolyn Lieberg, and the late Carl Klaus, the founder of the nonfiction writing program at the University of Iowa—read drafts of several chapters and provided incisive, valuable criticism. To all those people I offer my heartfelt thanks. I couldn't have done it without them. At the same time, of course, they are not responsible for the content of this book or any errors contained in it. That and those are solely mine.

Made in the USA
Middletown, DE
31 October 2023

41639023R00146